U.S. Fish & Wildlife Service

A Review of the Status of Greater and Lesser Scaup In North America

Note: Due to the complexity of some of the graphics and equations in this report, not all converted to portable document format clearly. We are working on correcting this problem. Scroll to next page to view report.

U.S. Fish and Wildlife Service

A REVIEW OF THE STATUS
OF GREATER AND LESSER
SCAUP IN NORTH AMERICA

A REVIEW OF THE STATUS OF GREATER

AND LESSER SCAUP IN NORTH AMERICA

George T. Allen, David F. Caithamer, and Mark Otto

Office of Migratory Bird Management
U.S. Fish and Wildlife Service
4401 North Fairfax Drive, Suite 634
Arlington, Virginia 22203-1610

JULY 1999

EXECUTIVE SUMMARY

The combined population of greater scaup (Aythya marila) and lesser scaup (Aythya affinis) in North America has declined substantially in recent years. In 1998 it reached the lowest level recorded since the start of systematic North American surveys in 1955. Concern about the numbers of scaup prompted this review of the status of the two species.

Our objective was to estimate linear trends in several measures of greater and lesser scaup abundance in North America. Those measures were (1) the annual spring Waterfowl Breeding Population and Habitat Surveys, (2) information on harvest in the United States and in Canada, (3) the annual Midwinter Waterfowl Survey, and (4) data from Christmas Bird Counts. We suspected that special seasons for scaup that ended in 1987 might have affected the populations. Therefore, we assessed trends for the period in which special regulations were used and for the period since then.

Spring surveys have indicated that the combined population of greater and lesser scaup declined from 1955 through 1998. There was no trend during 1955–1987, but there was a significant decline from 1988 through 1998. Surveys in areas we believe contain mostly greater scaup revealed no population trend during 1955–1998. Lesser scaup declined about 1% per year from 1955 through 1998. The number of lesser scaup has declined in 12 of the years since since 1983. In the boreal forest strata the population declined at about 6% per year. In the Yukon and Northwest Territories the population decline has been about 5% per year, in Alberta the decline has been about 7% per year, and in Manitoba and Ontario the decline has been about 10% per year.

The harvest of greater scaup in the U.S. has declined since 1961, though it increased from 1988 through 1998. We detected no trend in the age ratio of harvested scaup. We found no trend in the harvest of lesser scaup in the U.S. from 1961–1997, but the age ratio in the harvest declined about 1% per year. Also, the ratio of males to females in the lesser scaup harvest in the U.S. has increased; survival of lesser scaup females may have declined during the period for which data are available.

The harvest of greater scaup in Canada declined from 1974 through 1998. We detected no trend in the age ratio in the harvest; the mean was 2.51 immatures/adult. The harvest of lesser scaup in Canada declined, but we detected no trend in the age ratio in the harvest.

The harvest of all scaup in the United States and Canada declined from 1974 through 1997. We detected no trend in the proportion of the harvest taken in Canada or the U.S.

Midwinter surveys indicated that the number of scaup in the U.S. declined from 1955 through 1997. However, substantial variability in methods and state participation in the surveys reduce their value for population assessment.

Christmas Bird Count (CBC) data for all scaup indicated a decline in the Great Lakes region from 1955 through 1995, though during 1988–1995 the population increased. Greater scaup declined 3.2% per year during 1955–1995 because of declines in the numbers observed in the Atlantic Flyway and on the Great Lakes. However, greater scaup numbers increased in the Atlantic Flyway during 1988–1995. The CBC count total for lesser scaup from 1955 through 1995 indicated no change in the population.

Termination of special scaup hunting opportunities in 1988 did not produce a decrease in harvest or an increase in the lesser scaup spring population. Lesser scaup harvest appears to have responded more to season lengths and bag limits of the regular duck season.

After assessing trends, we developed and compared mathematical models of lesser scaup population dynamics to better understand factors affecting the size of the population and to aid harvest management. Our modeling revealed different inferences on the effect of hunting on lesser scaup, depending on the period assessed. For the period 1961 through 1998, we detected no relationship between fall harvest and the population the following spring. However, for the time since 1983 (when lesser scaup numbers began a consistent decline), we detected a negative relationship between U.S. harvest and subsequent population size; since 1983 hunting may have negatively affected the scaup populations. We believe that the results from the more recent time period are more representative of what will likely occur in the next several years.

Summary Table. Linear trends (P<0.1) of indices to scaup populations in North America.

Population index	Trend		
	Lesser scaup	Greater scaup	All scaup
1955–1998			
Spring population	Decline	No Trend	Decline
U.S. harvest (1961–1997)	No Trend	Decline	–
Canadian harvest (1974–1997)	Decline	Decline	–
Total harvest (1974–1997)	Decline	Decline	–
U.S. harvest age ratio (Immatures/adult) (1961–1997)	Decline	No Trend	
U.S. harvest sex ratio (males/female) (1969–1997)	No Trend	Increase	–
Canadian harvest age ratio (immatures/adult) (1969–1997)	No Trend	No Trend	–
Mid–winter Index[1]	–	–	Decline
Christmas Bird Counts (1955–1995)	No Trend	Decline	No Trend
1955–1987			
Spring population	No Trend	No Trend	No Trend
U.S. harvest (1961–1987)	No Trend	No Trend	–
Canadian harvest (1974–1987)	Decline	Decline	–
Total harvest (1974–1987)	No Trend	Decline	–
U.S. harvest age ratio (immatures/adult) (1961–1987)	Decline	No Trend	–
Canadian harvest age ratio (immatures/adult) (1969–1987)	No Trend	No Trend	
Mid–winter Index	–	–	Decline
Christmas Bird Counts	No Trend	Decline	No Trend
1988–1998			
Spring population	Decline	Increase	Decline
U.S. harvest (1988–1997)	Increase	Increase	–
Canadian harvest (1988–1987)	Decline	Decline	–
Total harvest (1988–1997)	Increase	No Trend	–
U.S. harvest age ratio (immatures/adult) (1988–1997)	No Trend	No Trend	–
Canadian harvest age ratio (immatures/adult) (1988–1997)	No Trend	No Trend	–
Mid–winter Index	–	–	No Trend
Christmas Bird Counts (1988–1995)	No Trend	No Trend	No Trend

[1] Midwinter counts for this analysis did not include data from surveys in Mexico.

INTRODUCTION

Recent trends in population levels of greater scaup (Aythya marila) and lesser scaup (Aythya affinis) concern wildlife managers in North America (Barclay and Zingo 1993, Caithamer and Smith 1995, Canadian Wildlife Service Waterfowl Committee 1998, Hodges et al. 1996, Wilkins et al. 1998). The number of breeding scaup has not met the North American Waterfowl Management Plan (U.S. Fish and Wildlife Service 1986, 1994) objective of 6,300,000 birds since 1984. Declines in the numbers of breeding greater scaup in Iceland, the western palearctic, and Ireland and Britain also are suggested by recent data (Kirby et al. 1993, Laursen 1989).

The greater scaup (Aythya marila marila) nests in Iceland and from northern Europe and Scandinavia to northern Siberia. Aythya marila nearctica (earlier called Aythya marila mariloides) nests across the arctic and subarctic in Alaska, the Yukon, the and Northwest Territories and, in lower numbers, east to the southern shores of Hudson Bay and to Lake Winnipeg. The majority of North American greater scaup nest in western and northern coastal Alaska and along the Beaufort Sea (Bellrose 1980, Johnson and Grier 1988, Palmer 1976; Figure 1). There are occasional movements of greater scaup between North America and Asia (Banks 1986).

The breeding range of the lesser scaup is much larger, from Minnesota to northeastern California, and north to central Alaska and Hudson Bay (Figure 2). It is .one of the more extensive breeding ranges of North American ducks. (Bellrose 1980). There is overlap of the nesting ranges of greater and lesser scaup, and it is rarely possible for observers in aerial surveys to distinguish between the species.

In winter, greater scaup concentrate in coastal areas whereas lesser scaup use both inland and coastal areas (Figures 3, and 4). About 60% of North American greater scaup winter on the East Coast, 20% on the Pacific Coast, and the rest winter in the interior U.S. and in the Gulf of Mexico (Bellrose 1980, Johnsgard 1975). Recent Christmas Bird Counts have indicated that most lesser scaup winter in the Atlantic and Mississippi Flyways, with smaller numbers found in the Central and Pacific Flyways. Some lesser scaup also winter as far south as northern South America and the West Indies (Bellrose 1980, Jewel 1913, Palmer 1976).

Bellrose (1980), McKnight and Buss (1962), Palmer (1976), and Trauger (1971) indicated that the majority of greater and lesser scaup first nest at two years old, although yearlings are capable of breeding. Bellrose (1980) also reported that the numbers of nonbreeding male lesser scaup found in flocks in late spring and early summer also indicate that most do not breed their first year. Austin et al. (1998) reported that lesser scaup can breed at one year of age, but ....the proportion of nonbreeding pairs varies with female age and water conditions..

Clapp et al. (1982) reported that the maximum recorded life span for both greater and lesser scaup is 18 years, 4 months. We found a recovery record of a lesser scaup that lived at least 20 years.

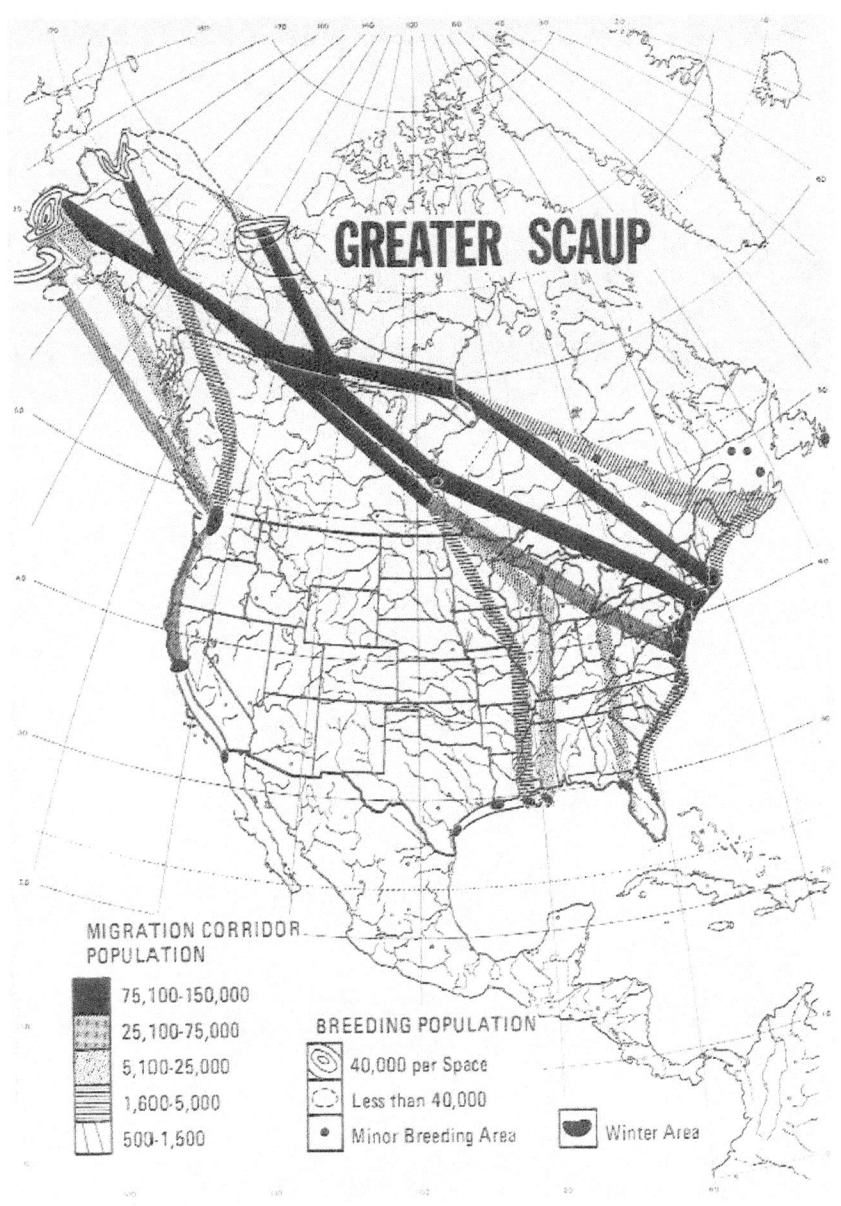

Figure 1. Breeding and wintering areas and major migration corridors of greater scaup in North America. From Bellrose (1980); reproduced by permission of the Wildlife Management Institute.

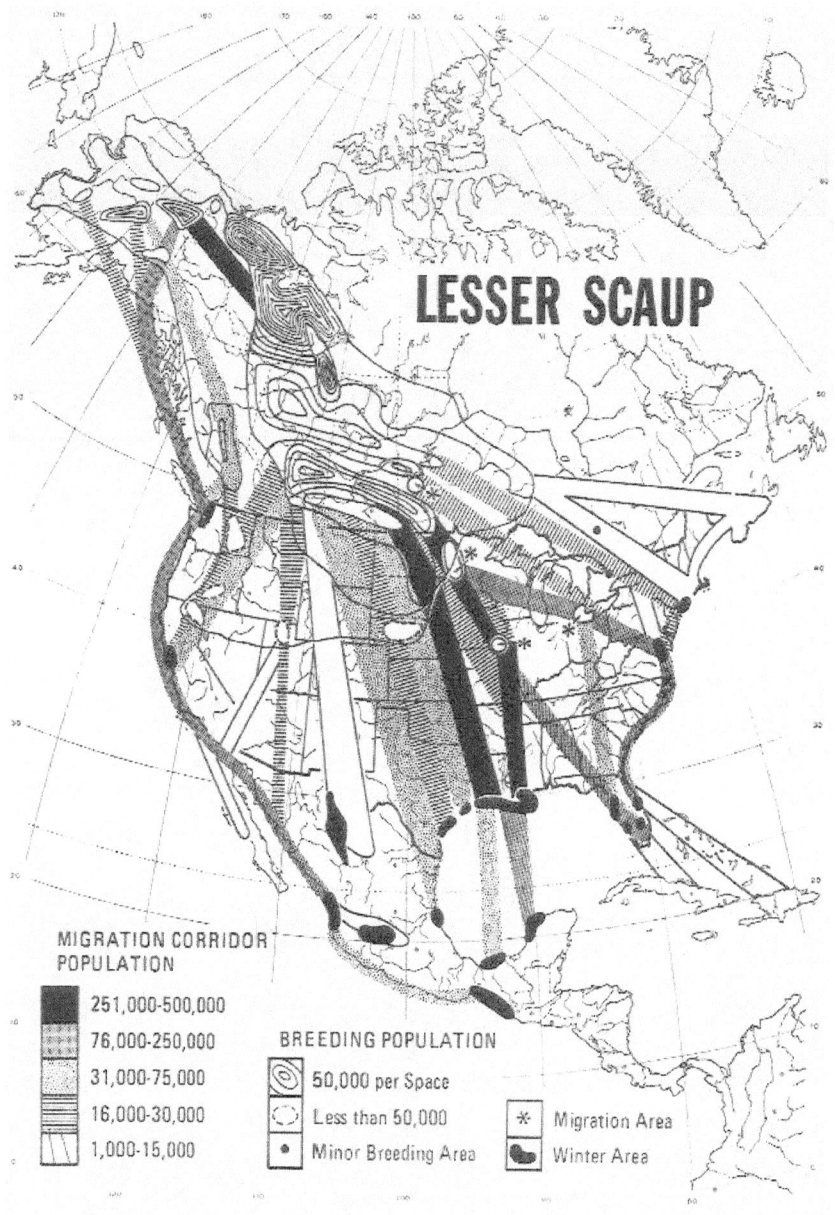

Figure 2. Breeding and wintering areas and major migration corridors of lesser scaup in North America. From Bellrose (1980); reproduced by permission of the Wildlife Management Institute.

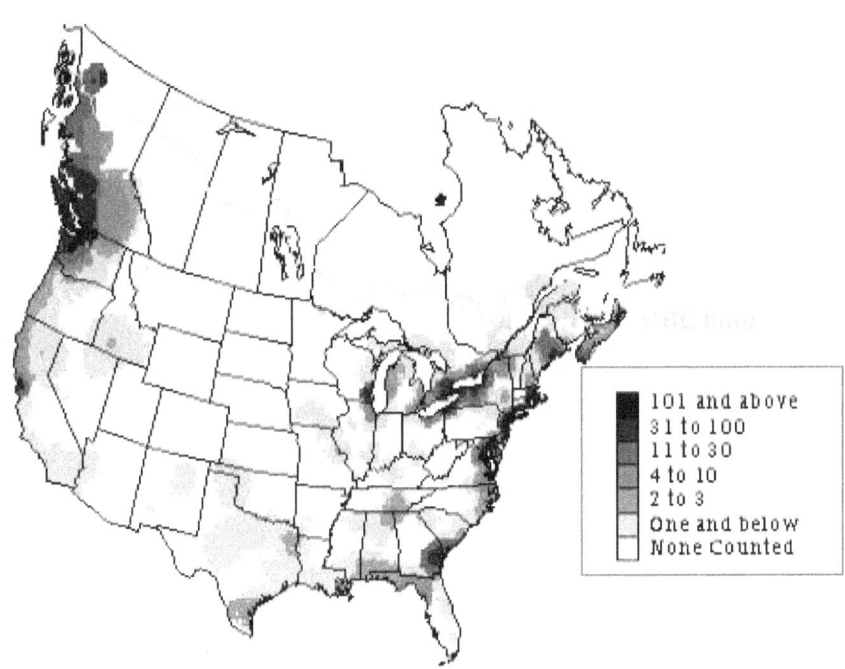

Figure 3. Average number of greater scaup on recent Christmas Bird Counts. From Sauer et al. (1996).

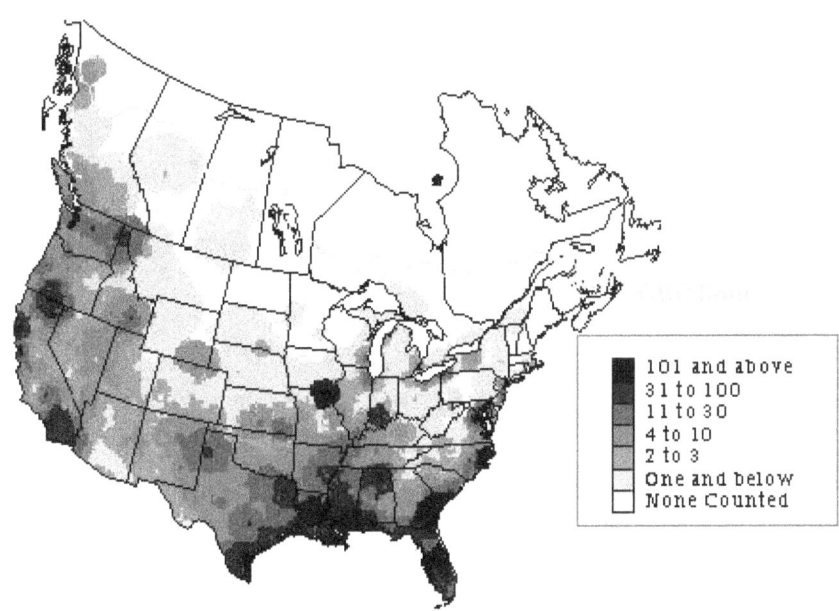

Figure 4. Average number of lesser scaup on recent Christmas Bird Counts. From Sauer et al. (1996).

OBJECTIVES

The primary objective of our evaluation was to assess continent-wide measures of scaup status and trends. We evaluated three measures of population abundance: spring population estimates, mid-winter counts, and Christmas Bird Counts. We also examined harvest estimates from the United States and from Canada, and age ratios in the U.S. and Canadian harvests, which we considered indices of recruitment. When possible, we tested for trends for the period 1955 through 1998. However, several of the surveys did not begin until after 1955. For example, U.S. harvest estimates were not available prior to 1961.

We suspected that special scaup seasons and bonus bag limits may have had discernible effects on harvest and populations. Therefore, we described trends for the periods in which extra harvest was possible (prior to 1988) and in the time since then.

Lastly, we wished to develop mathematical models describing the dynamics of lesser scaup numbers. We were particularly interested in the role of U.S. harvest. We modeled the data for 1961 through 1998, and for the period of steady decline in the lesser scaup population — 1983 through 1998.

SCAUP HUNTING SEASONS AND REGULATIONS IN THE U.S.

Bonus scaup Bag Limits

In the early 1960s scaup were identified as a lightly harvested species that could provide additional hunting opportunities. In 1962, a bonus bag limit that permitted taking two scaup in addition to the regular daily bag limit was offered to the three eastern Flyways. Bonus birds were allowed in areas mutually agreed upon by states and the U.S. Fish and Wildlife Service. Bonus scaup limits could not be used until after 1 November, and states that selected the point system were ineligible for the scaup bonus. Bonus scaup limits were discontinued in 1964 due to the extensive illegal harvest of ring-necked ducks (Aythya collaris) that were misidentified as scaup. However, the bonus limits were reinstated in 1965 in states that selected harvest areas where there were few ring-necks during the bonus period. In 1966, ring-necks were permitted in the bonus bag; but they were dropped the following year out of concern for their status. The bonus scaup limit was discontinued in 1988 due to concern over the general status of ducks and wetland conditions in the prairie-pothole region.

Special Scaup Seasons

As early as 1963, the Atlantic Flyway Council considered the use of a special scaup season in lieu of the bonus bag limit option. The first special scaup season was initiated in 1966 in Long Island Sound. New York and Connecticut were permitted to select a 15-day period outside the regular duck season and offered aggregate scaup and ring-neck bag and possession limits of 5 and 10, respectively. The ring-necked duck was removed from the special-season regulations in 1967, due to its higher harvest rate compared to scaup and its uncertain population status. The season was expanded to include the Atlantic, Mississippi, and Central Flyways by 1968. Nineteen states participated in the special scaup seasons. These seasons were available until 1988, when they were suspended by the Service.

In the Atlantic Flyway, the bonus scaup limits were in place in every state during the 1962–63 and 1963–64 seasons. Thereafter, either a bonus bag limit or a special season for scaup was used in most states in the Flyway each year.

In the Mississippi Flyway, the scaup bonus, when available, was selected by most states through the early 1970s. Thereafter, the special scaup season was selected in most years by Indiana, Louisiana, Michigan, Ohio, and Wisconsin.

Special regulations for scaup were seldom selected in the Central Flyway. Most of the Central Flyway states selected the scaup bonus in 1962–63. After that season, North Dakota selected the bonus in 1987–88. Oklahoma selected either the bonus or the special season from 1969–70 through 1972–73, and South Dakota selected the special season in 1969–70 and the bonus in 1970–71.

METHODS

We used five measures to assess population trends for the two species.

1) <u>Waterfowl Breeding Population and Habitat Surveys</u>. Each May and June since 1955, an aerial survey of breeding waterfowl populations is conducted in portions of the United States and Canada. The survey area encompasses the principal breeding areas for ducks in North America, and is subdivided into 59 strata (Figure 5). The aerial counts are adjusted for visibility bias to yield annual population estimates. In southern areas concurrent ground counts provide the visibility adjustments. In northern areas, helicopter counts done from 1986 through 1988 are used to make visibility adjustments.

The timing and coverage of the surveys are oriented primarily at mallards (Anas platyrhynchos). Because their migration is protracted, scaup may not be surveyed as well. Diving ducks also are less affected by variability in wetland conditions than are dabbling ducks, and scaup numbers in the surveys are not closely associated with pond numbers (Johnson and Grier 1988). Despite these limitations, we believe the breeding population survey is the best long-term index for scaup in North America.

The survey protocol requires that the observers not attempt to distinguish between greater and lesser scaup. For our analyses we relied on information in Bellrose (1980) and Hodges et al. (1996), and assumed that scaup found in tundra habitats in Alaska and the Northwest Territories (strata 8, 9, 10, 11, and 13) are primarily greater scaup and those in other strata are primarily lesser scaup. This method is supported by information from banding efforts (Table 1, Figure 6) which reveal that more than 95% of the scaup banded in Alaska tundra strata were greater scaup; whereas in non-tundra strata, more than 95% were lesser scaup. Subjective judgments by field biologists in the Northwest Territories and Alaska (A. Aderman, M. Bertram, D. Kay, B. Larned, B. Skinner, M. Spindler, D. Troy, and M. Vivion, personal communications) also indicated that 95 to 100 percent of the scaup in tundra areas were greater scaup, and that 75 to more than 90% of scaup in most other strata were lesser scaup. However, B. Kessel

Figure 5. Transects and strata of the breeding waterfowl and habitat survey.

reported that in the 1950s at Minto Lake in stratum 3 the split was about 50% greater scaup and 50% lesser scaup (M. Spindler, personal communication).

We were concerned that several of the spring population estimates may have been biased high, a possible result of conducting the surveys during the scaup spring migration. We suspected that double–counting was most likely to have occurred if a survey was conducted too early or if it was protracted. Lacking a direct measure of double–counting, we tested for linear relationships between the log of the g population estimate of lesser scaup and descriptive statistics from the survey. We looked for a relationship between average survey date and the size of the population. We also tested the hypothesis that more protracted surveys would produce greater estimates. If scaup were still migrating, during any spring count, we assumed that they would tend to be counted in larger groups (five or more birds) on the more southerly strata. Consequently, so we tested the relationship between the proportion of the scaup that were grouped and the size of the breeding population. If large numbers of scaup were migrating during the survey, we also assumed that the average latitude of their distribution would be more southerly and the variance of the latitude would be large compared to years when few scaup were still migrating.

Table 1. Distribution of summer bandings during 1925–1996 of greater and lesser scaup in North America relative to the Spring population survey.

Region	Survey Area	Number banded		Percent Greater Scaup
		Greater scaup	Lesser scaup	
Alaska	Tundra strata	2787	41	98.6
	Non-tundra strata	435	32203	1.3
	Unsurveyed	117	404	22.5
Yukon and Northwest Territories	Tundra strata	0	0	
	Non-tundra strata	129	5156	2.4
	Unsurveyed	35	93	27.3
British Columbia, Alberta, Saskatchewan, and Manitoba	Surveyed	41	36738	0.1
	Unsurveyed	219	3612	5.7
Montana, North Dakota, and South Dakota	Surveyed	8	1247	0.6
	Unsurveyed	0	565	0.0

The 1977 change in the airplane type used in the surveys in Alaska produced an .artificial and instantaneous increase in the populations-size index of all species of ducks. (Hodges et al. 1996). Visibility of waterfowl was much improved when the newer type plane was brought into use; and the average increase in numbers observed was 26% for all duck species combined. The visibility change was less significant for greater scaup than for lesser scaup. Though Alaska data for years prior to 1977 could be adjusted, annual variability in greater scaup numbers, and often in lesser scaup numbers appears to have been greater than the visibility bias. We used the survey data from Wilkins et al. (1998), which do not include any visibility corrections for Alaska counts.

2) Band Recoveries. Recoveries of bands can provide information to estimate rates of harvest, survival, and movement. However, for lesser scaup banded in the summer, direct recoveries have averaged less than five per year and indirect recoveries have averaged less than four per year since 1971 (Table 2). There have been far fewer recoveries for greater scaup. These recoveries are insufficient for estimating survival or recovery rates.

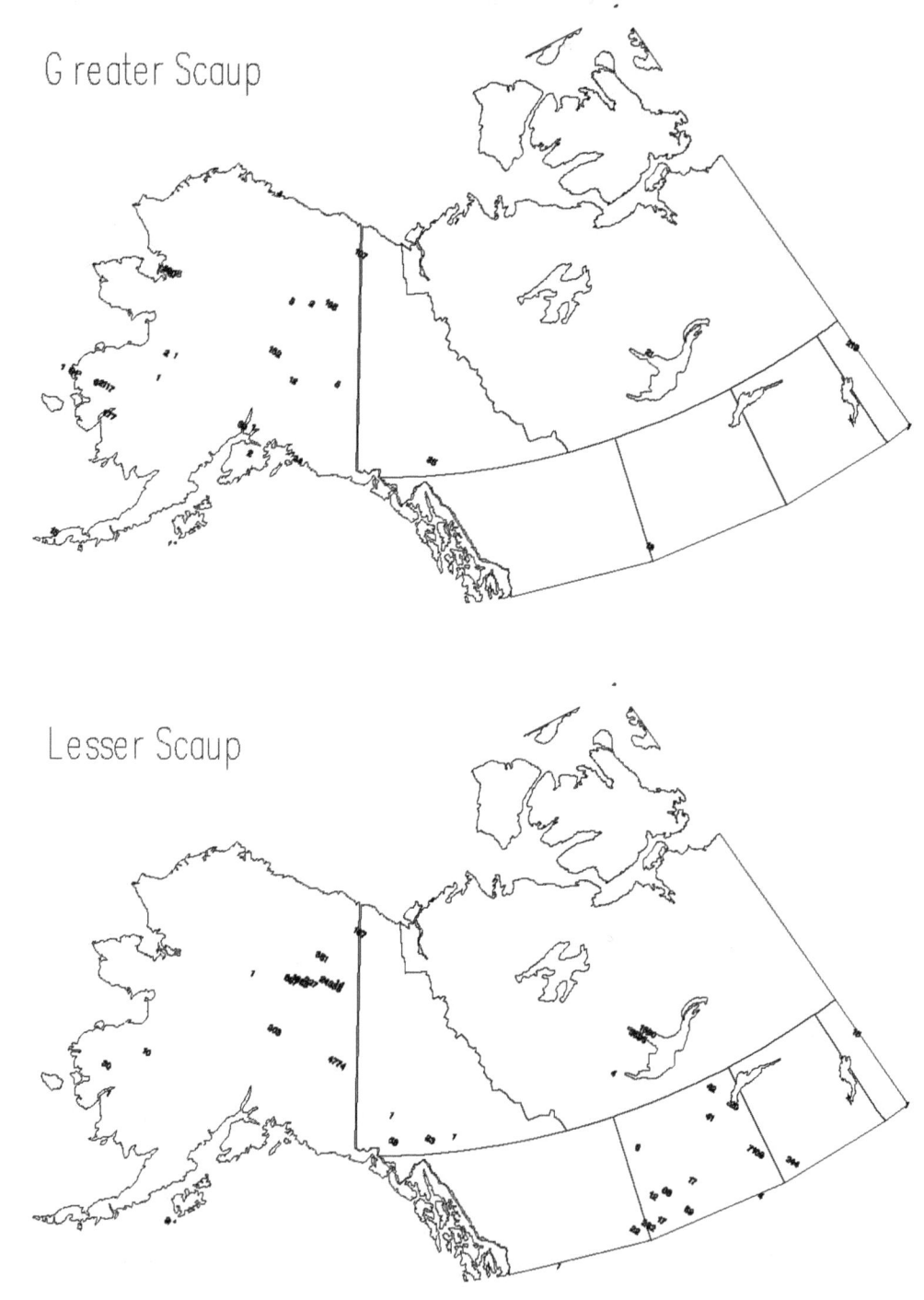

Figure 6. Numbers and locations of scaup banded during summer in northwestern North America, 1925-1996.

Table 2. Total recoveries each decade of bands from scaup banded during the summer and recovered during hunting seasons, 1951 through 1995. Data from the U.S. Geological Survey, Biological Resources Division, Bird Banding Laboratory, September 1997 (personal communication).

| Banding period | Band recoveries | | | | | | | | | |
| | Immature females | | Immature males | | Adult females | | Adult males | | Total | |
	Direct	Indirect	Direct	Indirect	Direct	Indirect	Direct	Indirect	Direct	Indirect
Greater scaup										
1951–1959	25	8	19	15	2	1	45	0	47	24
1960–1969	0	1	0	0	1	8	25	124	26	133
1970–1979	1	0	0	1	0	4	0	2	1	7
1980–1989	0	0	0	0	0	4	0	0	0	4
1990–1995	2	0	0	0	0	0	2	0	4	0
Lesser scaup										
1951–1959	190	68	238	91	27	29	46	62	501	250
1960–1969	332	135	439	183	67	104	465	1338	1303	1760
1970–1979	39	25	35	28	5	6	5	5	84	64
1980–1989	28	17	16	7	2	2	2	5	48	31
1990–1995	8	3	3	3	3	3	4	7	18	16

3) Harvest. Hunter surveys provide estimates of scaup harvest, age and sex composition of the harvest, hunter numbers, and hunting efforts (Martin and Carney 1977). Harvest may reflect numbers of scaup available to hunters; age ratios (ratios of young to adults) in the harvest may be indexes to recruitment rates; and sex ratios (ratios of males to females) may indicate changes in survival of males or females. We evaluated trends in all three population measures. However, there were insufficient data to calculate sex ratios in the Central Flyway harvest of greater scaup.

4) Midwinter Surveys. The Midwinter Waterfowl Survey has been conducted since the 1930s in some states, usually in the first full working week in January. Eggeman and Johnson (1989) and Montalbano et al. (1985) determined that the variability in Midwinter Survey methods across states and time periods made population comparisons questionable. The variety in methods makes statistical variation in the counts unmeasurable, and the many variables involved greatly influence the proportion of waterfowl counted (Eggeman et al. 1997). We consider the Midwinter Survey a less reliable indicator of population levels than the breeding population survey. However, it provides considerable information about relative numbers and distribution.

5) Christmas Bird Counts. National Audubon Society Christmas Bird Counts are coordinated efforts conducted in December throughout the U.S. and parts of Canada, Mexico, and Central America. Each count is a survey of a 15-mile-diameter circle (Sauer et al. 1996). The

number of birds counted is a function of effort, and there is much variation in participant numbers and effort expended on each survey. Approximately 1600 survey areas contained scaup during 1955–1995. After standardizing the CBC data for observer effort, J. Sauer (U.S. Geological Survey Biological Resources Division, personal communication) estimated population trends for greater and lesser scaup in several regions of North America. CBC observer skills, weather conditions, and survey intensity vary by year and location. We consider the information from the CBCs less reliable for indicating population trends than the breeding population survey.

We log-transformed data from these indicators when they were not normally distributed, and trends were assessed using linear regression with $\alpha=0.1$. We analyzed data for periods through spring 1988, after summer 1988, and for the full periods for which data were available. Finally, to aid our assessment of management needs, we developed models of the population dynamics of lesser scaup to better assess the possible effects of hunting.

RESULTS

SPRING WATERFOWL SURVEYS

Spring populations of scaup varied substantially during 1955–1998 (Tables 3 and 4). On average, the scaup population declined ($P=0.008$) about 0.6% per year during 1955–1998. In tundra strata, which probably contain mostly greater scaup, no trend was evident during this period. During 1988–1998, lesser scaup estimates declined nearly 3% per year, while estimates of greater scaup trended upwards about 4% per year (Figure 7). In strata that we believe contained mostly lesser scaup and few greater scaup, the population has varied considerably, but on average declined 0.6% per year during 1955–1998 (Figure 8). In all strata combined, estimates of scaup decreased about 2% per year during 1988–1998.

We found differences in the breeding population trends from 1955 through 1998 in the different habitat types in which scaup nest. In tundra strata (greater scaup strata, 8–11 and 13) and prairie strata (26–49), the population increased slightly. However, in the boreal forest (strata 1–7, 14–25, 50, and 75–77) the population declined at about 6% per year. In the Yukon and Northwest Territories (strata 12 and 14 through 18), the population decline has been about 5% per year. In Alberta (strata 20 and 75 through 77), the decline has been about 7% per year. In Saskatchewan (strata 21, 22, and 23) there was no significant trend. In the Manitoba and Ontario boreal forest strata (24, 25, and 50), the decline has been about 10% per year.

Table 3. Scaup population estimates from spring breeding surveys, 1955–1998. From Wilkins et al. (1998).

Year	Population estimate	Standard error of the estimate	Year	Population estimate	Standard error of the estimate
1955	5,620,100	582,100	1977	6,260,200	362,800
1956	5,994,100	434,000	1978	5,984,400	403,000
1957	5,766,900	411,700	1979	7,657,900	548,600
1958	5,350,400	355,100	1980	6,381,700	421,200
1959	7,037,600	492,300	1981	5,990,900	414,200
1960	4,868,600	362,500	1982	5,532,000	380,900
1961	5,380,000	442,200	1983	7,173,800	494,900
1962	5,286,100	426,400	1984	7,024,300	484,700
1963	5,438,400	357,900	1985	5,098,000	333,100
1964	5,131,800	386,100	1986	5,235,300	355,500
1965	4,640,000	411,200	1987	4,862,700	303,800
1966	4,439,200	356,200	1988	4,671,400	309,500
1967	4,927,700	456,100	1989	4,342,100	291,300
1968	4,412,700	351,800	1990	4,293,100	264,900
1969	5,139,800	378,500	1991	5,254,900	364,900
1970	5,662,500	391,400	1992	4,639,200	291,900
1971	5,143,300	333,800	1993	4,080,100	249,400
1972	7,997,000	718,000	1994	4,529,000	253,600
1973	6,257,400	523,100	1995	4,446,400	277,600
1974	5,780,500	409,800	1996	4,217,400	234,500
1975	6,460,000	486,000	1997	4,112,300	224,200
1976	5,818,700	348,700	1998	3,471,900	191,200

Table 4. Results of linear regression modeling of natural log-transformed estimates of scaup breeding populations in North America, 1955–1997.

Area	Survey period	Population change per year	P (Slope=0)
	1955–1987	0.004	0.162
All strata	1988–1998	−0.019	0.043
	1955–1998	−0.006	0.008
	1955–1987	−0.001	0.838
Tundra strata (greater scaup)[1]	1988–1998	0.044	0.031
	1955–1998	0.002	0.397
	1955–1987	0.003	0.313
Other strata (lesser scaup)[2]	1988–1998	−0.027	0.007
	1955–1998	−0.006	0.005

[1] Strata 8, 9, 10, 11, and 13.
[2] Strata 1–7, 12, 14–18, 20–50, and 75–77.

There was a significant relationship between average survey date and the size of the population, but average survey date explained only about 12% (adjusted r–square) of the variation in breeding population size. Also, the five years with the highest counts had average survey dates that were similar to those for the other years (t–test, P=0.95). There was no relationship between the span of the survey and the size of the population (P=0.13), so there was no evidence that more protracted surveys would produce greater estimates. Nor was there any no relationship between the proportion of the scaup that were grouped and the size of the breeding population (P=0.79). Average latitude of the scaup distribution during the Spring Surveys was not related to size of the breeding population (P=0.67). The relationship between variance of the latitude was very significant (P=0.0001), but in the direction opposite from what we expected. Scaup population estimates tended to be highest when the birds were most concentrated, and estimates tended to be lower in years when the birds were more uniformly dispersed during the surveys. We concluded that there is only weak evidence that the high population estimates were biased.

HARVEST
Harvest and Age Ratios in the United States
The harvest of greater scaup in the U.S. declined from 1961 through 1997 (P=0.001, Table 5, Figures 9 and 10). The age ratio in the harvest has not changed significantly since 1961 (P=0.212).

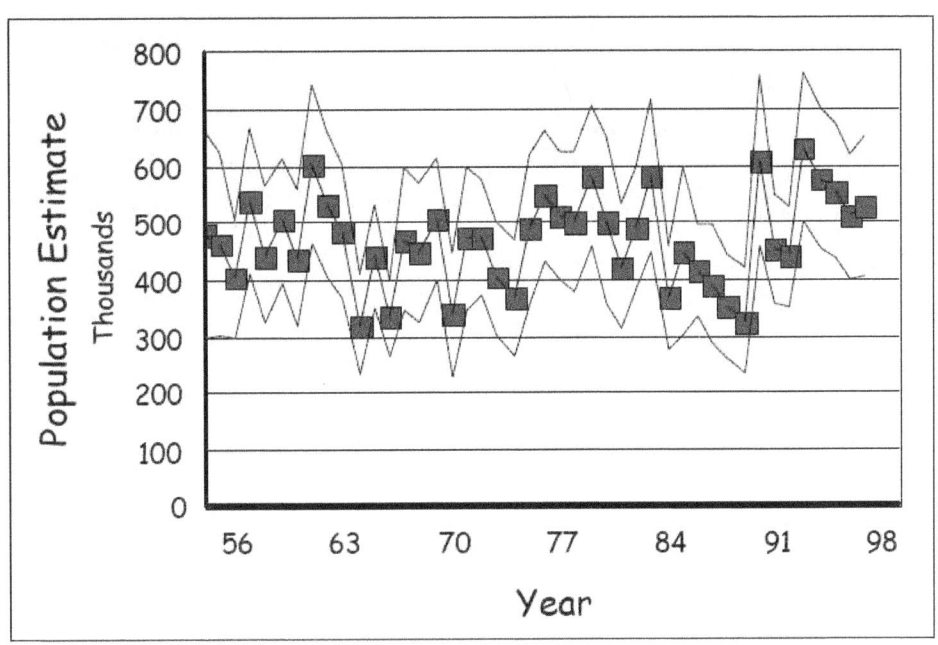

Figure 7. Greater scaup (strata 8, 9, 10, 11, and 13) breeding population estimates and 95% confidence interval from the Spring Surveys, 1955-1998.

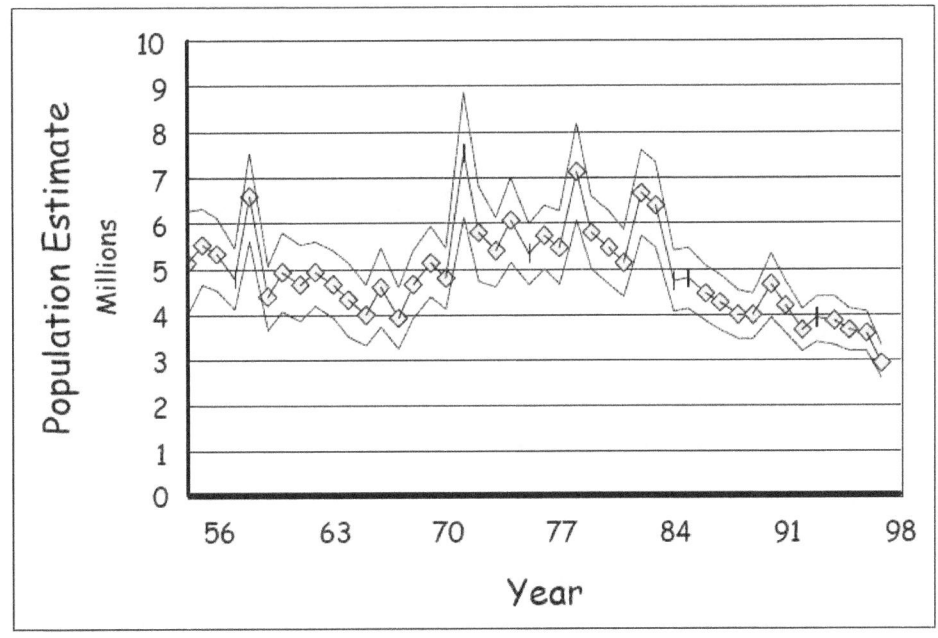

Figure 8. Lesser scaup (strata 1-7, 12, 14-18, 20-50, and 75-77) breeding population estimates and 95% confidence intervals from the Spring Surveys, 1955-1998.

Table 5. Estimates of scaup harvest, age composition of the harvest, and waterfowl hunter efforts in the U.S., 1961–1997. Data from P. Padding (USFWS, MBMO), (personal communications).

| Hunting season | Greater scaup | | Lesser scaup | | Total scaup harvest | Hunter days |
	Harvest	Immatures per adult ratio	Harvest	Immatures per adult ratio		
1961	30,700	1.10	288,200	2.31	318,900	6,520,028
1962	73,600	1.76	93,300	1.43	166,900	6,084,842
1963	59,300	1.42	263,000	1.56	322,300	7,866,129
1964	49,000	1.33	314,000	1.55	363,000	9,207,618
1965	46,700	0.97	466,400	2.03	513,100	9,296,760
1966	89,900	1.95	473,500	2.32	563,400	11,556,862
1967	108,200	1.43	421,000	1.82	529,200	12,300,791
1968	78,300	1.07	179,100	1.38	257,400	10,386,513
1969	114,100	1.10	513,800	1.57	627,900	13,752,906
1970	111,500	0.90	354,800	1.48	466,300	17,065,282
1971	95,600	1.26	495,800	1.87	591,400	16,640,964
1972	127,800	1.52	479,100	1.57	606,900	15,184,059
1973	98,000	1.78	654,400	1.26	752,400	14,501,457
1974	65,800	1.13	450,700	1.35	516,500	15,337,884
1975	102,800	1.62	359,100	2.01	461,900	16,377,069
1976	88,900	1.59	535,000	1.94	623,900	15,306,948
1977	132,500	1.08	686,800	0.46	819,300	15,249,555
1978	61,000	1.50	316,900	1.17	377,900	15,629,168

Harvest of lesser scaup in the U.S. was variable (range 93,300 – 686,800), and no linear trend in harvest was apparent ($P=0.119$, Figures 11 and 12). However, the age ratio decreased ($P=0.01$) about 1% per year from 1961 through 1997.

Harvest and Sex Ratios in the United States

In the Atlantic and Mississippi Flyways and in the U.S., there have not been significant changes in the sex ratio in the harvest ($P=0.89$ in the Pacific Flyway, $P=0.20$ in the Mississippi Flyway, and $P=0.36$ in the U.S., Table 6, Figures 13 and 14). In the Pacific Flyway, there has been a gradual decline in the ratio of males to females since 1969 ($P=0.06$).

For lesser scaup, the trends have been different (Table 7, Figures 15 and 16). Though there has not been a significant change in the ration in the Pacific Flyway ($P=0.18$). However, there have been significant increases in the ratios of males to females in the harvest in the Atlantic ($P=0.07$), Mississippi ($P=0.05$), and Central ($P=0.02$) Flyways and in the U.S. ($P=0.03$).

Table 5 (continued). Estimates of scaup harvest, age composition of the harvest, and waterfowl hunter efforts in the U.S., 1961–1997. Data from P. Padding (USFWS, MBMO), (personal communications).

Hunting season	Greater scaup		Lesser scaup		Total scaup harvest	Hunter days
	Harvest	Immatures per adult ratio	Harvest	Immatures per adult ratio		
1979	40,700	1.57	254,100	1.87	294,800	15,358,389
1980	68,500	1.22	239,900	1.71	308,400	14,304,358
1981	125,700	1.05	550,000	0.86	675,700	13,341,838
1982	40,900	0.68	358,800	0.70	399,700	13,423,424
1983	75,000	1.70	272,700	1.66	347,700	12,367,882
1984	72,200	2.04	663,300	1.43	735,500	12,815,800
1985	65,600	0.99	488,300	1.09	553,900	10,874,364
1986	38,100	1.44	250,100	1.44	288,200	11,200,073
1987	45,900	1.46	187,000	1.66	232,900	10,482,003
1988	26,400	1.31	148,500	1.36	174,900	7,771,851
1989	26,400	1.40	127,800	1.58	154,200	8,312,917
1990	27,800	1.53	103,200	1.07	131,000	8,652,191
1991	19,100	1.22	152,500	1.49	171,600	8,898,679
1992	20,000	1.22	189,400	0.78	209,400	8,714,616
1993	27,200	2.23	107,500	1.31	134,700	9,300,339
1994	29,300	1.91	178,900	1.67	208,200	10,935,528
1995	53,900	1.56	285,900	1.12	339,800	12,217,852
1996	51,500	0.93	461,000	0.85	512,500	13,240,642
1997	63,600	2.06	511,100	1.28	631,600	14,944,061

The relative vulnerability of males and females to hunting may have changed over time. However, we believe it more likely that lesser scaup female survival may have declined during the period for which data are available. Among the possible reasons for such a decline are habitat changes that led to increased vulnerability of females to predators, and decreased survival of females due to the effects of contaminants.

Waterfowl Hunting Effort in the United States
Trends in the number of days spent waterfowl hunting in the Atlantic, Central, and Pacific Flyways have been similar since 1961 (Figure 17). The number of days expended in the Mississippi Flyway has been higher and has varied more (Figure 18). The harvest of scaup per hunter per day declined about 2% per year from 1961 through 1996 (P=0.001).

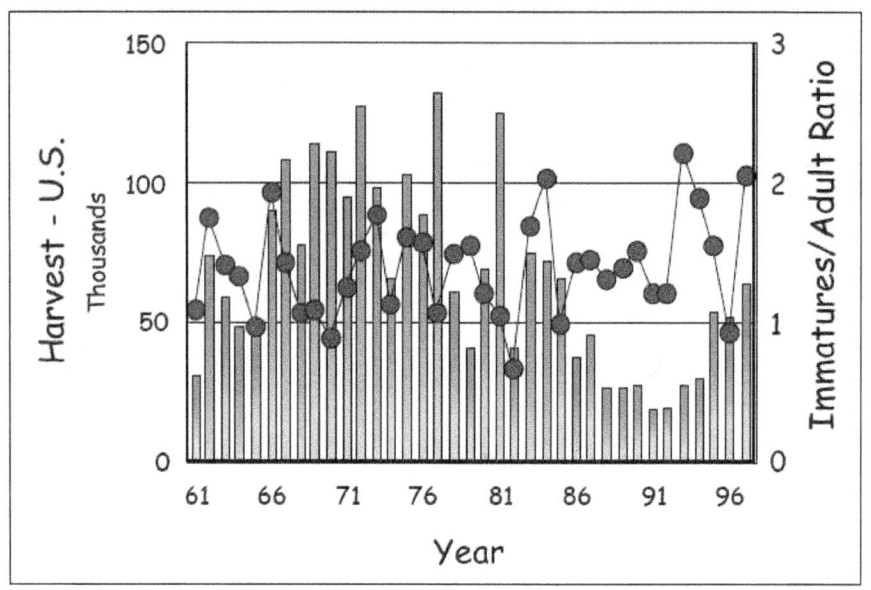

Figure 9. U.S. greater scaup harvest (bars) and immatures/adult age ratios (dots) in the harvest, 1961 through 1997. Data from P. Padding (USFWS, MBMO), (personal communication).

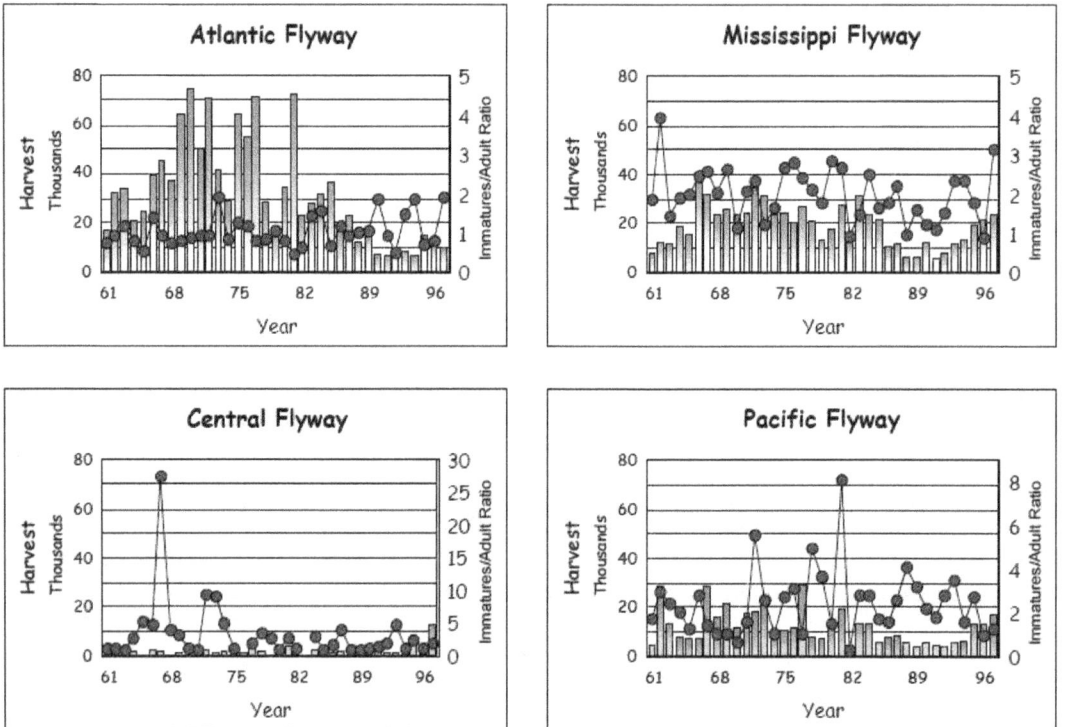

Figure 10. U.S. greater scaup harvest, 1961–1997 (bars) and immatures/adult ratios, 1961–1996 (dots) in the Flyways. Data from P. Padding (USFWS, MBMO), (personal communication).

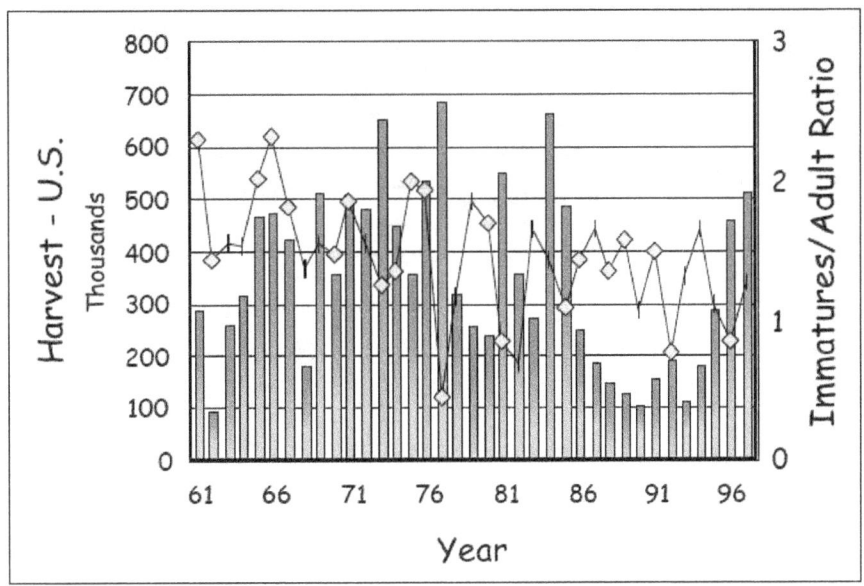

Figure 11. U.S. lesser scaup harvest (bars) and immatures/adult age ratios (diamonds) in the harvest, 1961 through 1997. Data from P. Padding (USFWS, MBMO), (personal communication).

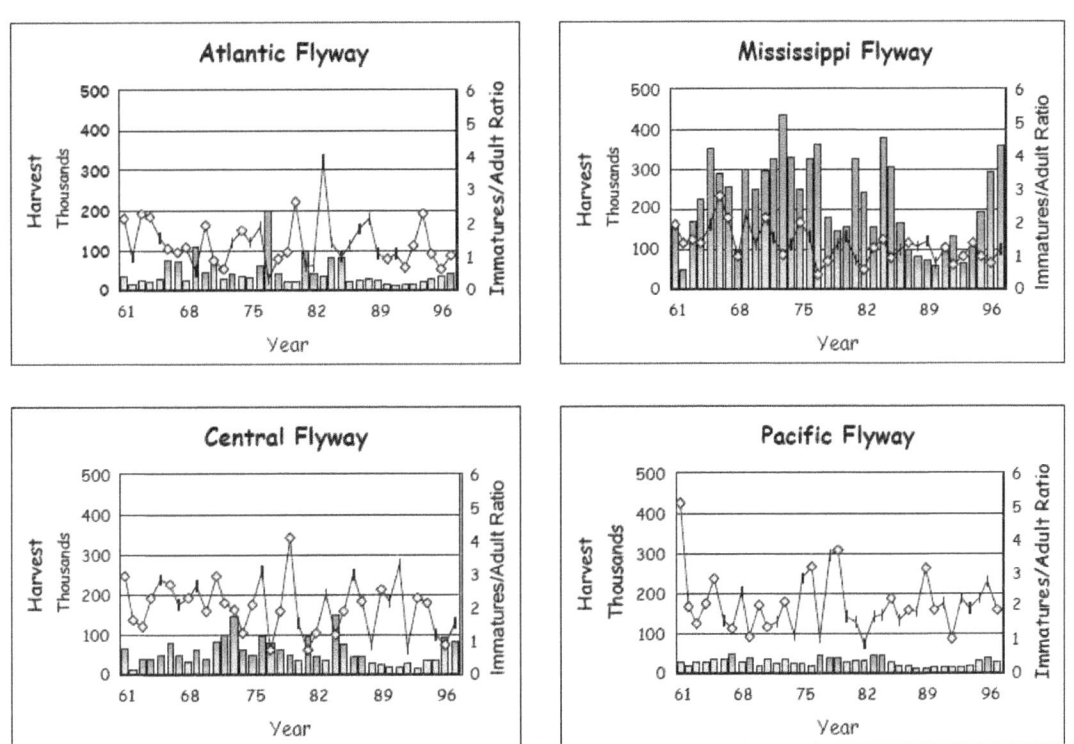

Figure 12. U.S. lesser scaup harvest, 1961–1997 (bars) and immatures/adult ratios, 1961–1996 (dots) in the Flyways. Data from P. Padding (USFWS, MBMO), (personal communication).

Table 6. Sex ratios (males/female) in the U.S. greater scaup harvest, 1969–1997. NC=Not calculated.

| Year | Flyway | | | U.S. |
	Atlantic	Mississippi	Pacific	
1969	1.13	0.85	0.90	0.97
1970	0.85	0.96	0.79	1.48
1971	0.90	0.79	1.49	0.84
1972	0.97	1.48	0.84	1.09
1973	0.95	1.31	1.34	1.09
1974	1.48	1.40	0.63	1.35
1975	0.89	0.89	0.63	0.85
1976	0.94	1.06	0.74	0.93
1977	0.99	0.95	0.64	0.90
1978	2.19	0.48	NC	1.32
1979	1.40	2.27	NC	1.54
1980	1.58	0.51	1.17	1.31
1981	1.51	0.55	NC	1.25
1982	1.82	1.65	1.44	1.73
1983	0.87	1.27	1.01	1.07
1984	0.97	0.71	0.86	0.81
1985	0.70	0.88	1.95	0.89
1986	0.90	0.96	0.89	0.91
1987	1.04	0.72	1.30	0.93
1988	0.79	0.33	1.29	0.82
1989	0.84	1.13	0.72	0.94
1990	0.97	2.11	1.05	1.38
1991	0.68	0.71	1.73	1.02
1992	0.78	0.74	1.55	0.94
1993	1.45	0.77	NC	0.94
1994	0.78	0.90	1.01	0.81
1995	1.26	0.69	0.97	0.91
1996	1.11	0.68	1.72	0.97
1997	1.74	0.62	1.93	1.25

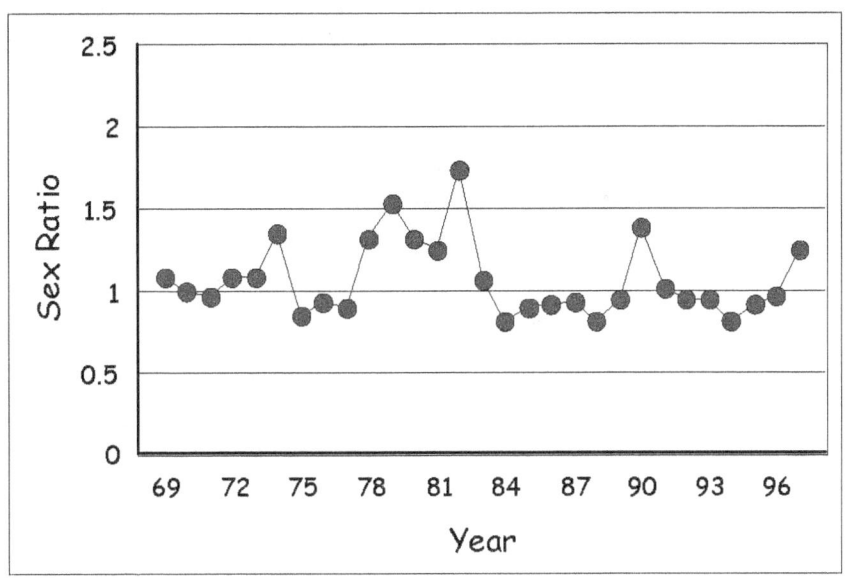

Figure 13. Sex ratios in the U.S. harvest of greater scaup, 1969 – 1997.

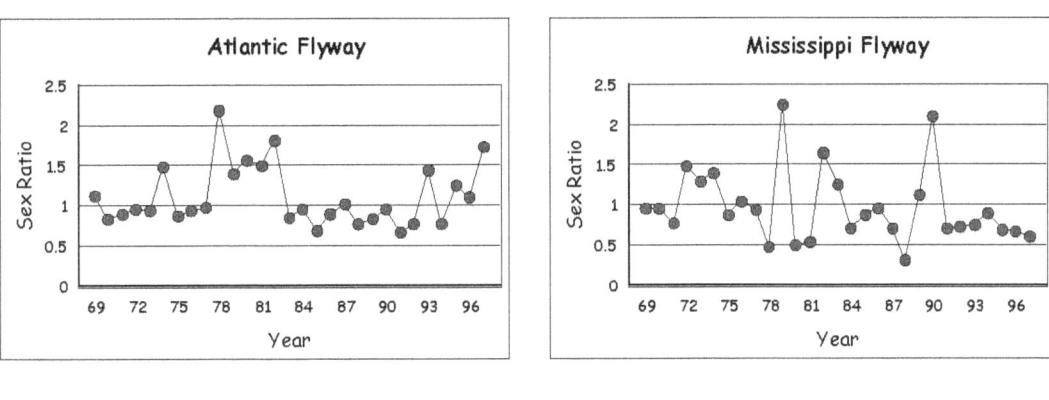

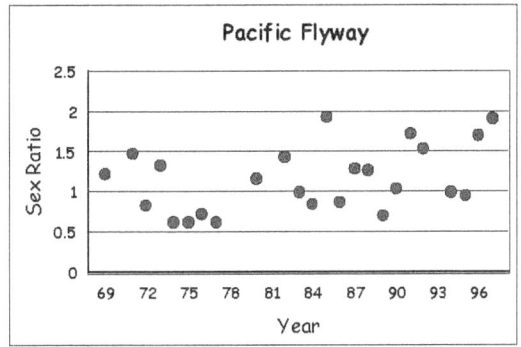

Figure 14. Sex ratios for the harvests of greater scaup in the Atlantic, Mississippi, and Pacific Flyways, 1969 – 1997. Sex ratio could not be calculated for some years in the Pacific Flyway.

Table 7. Sex ratios (males/female) in the U.S. lesser scaup harvest, 1969–1997.

Year	Flyway				U.S.
	Atlantic	Mississippi	Central	Pacific	
1969	1.08	1.22	1.10	1.08	1.17
1970	1.20	1.38	0.81	0.98	1.24
1971	1.65	1.07	1.27	1.36	1.17
1972	1.25	1.20	1.20	0.73	1.18
1973	0.82	1.30	1.45	1.00	1.28
1974	0.99	1.25	1.20	0.85	1.20
1975	1.08	1.30	1.26	0.82	1.22
1976	0.97	1.18	1.49	1.16	1.20
1977	2.61	1.79	1.26	1.00	1.70
1978	2.21	1.53	0.78	1.37	1.45
1979	1.54	1.79	1.17	2.66	1.74
1980	1.14	1.54	1.35	1.65	1.48
1981	2.41	2.04	1.25	2.20	1.91
1982	2.59	2.01	1.89	1.97	2.03
1983	0.75	1.41	0.94	0.94	1.12
1984	1.08	1.36	1.50	0.88	1.31
1985	1.06	1.19	1.16	1.07	1.15
1986	1.60	1.16	1.09	1.26	1.17
1987	0.80	1.52	1.44	1.01	1.31
1988	0.66	1.00	0.96	0.61	0.88
1989	1.11	1.07	1.01	0.62	1.02
1990	0.91	1.35	2.83	1.01	1.43
1991	1.24	1.17	1.44	1.08	1.20
1992	0.69	0.97	1.15	0.96	0.97
1993	1.66	1.83	1.21	2.58	1.78
1994	2.90	1.97	1.82	2.24	2.02
1995	2.54	1.67	1.54	1.76	1.73
1996	3.43	2.12	2.50	1.77	2.26
1997	2.67	2.33	1.50	1.23	2.14

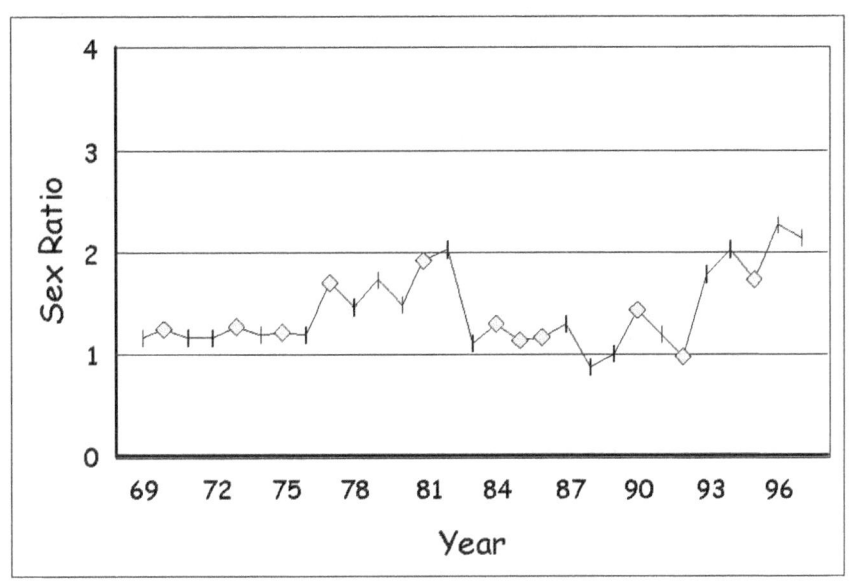

Figure 15. Sex ratios in the U.S. harvest of lesser scaup, 1969 – 1997.

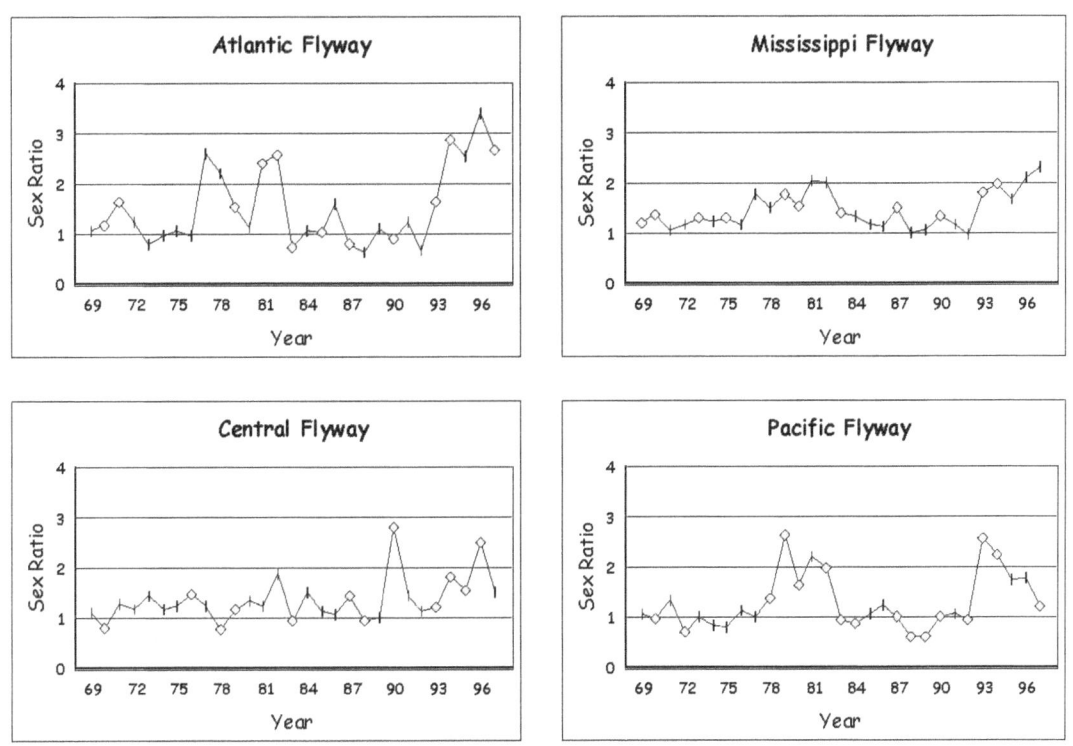

Figure 16. Sex ratios for the harvests of lesser scaup in the Flyways, 1969 – 1997.

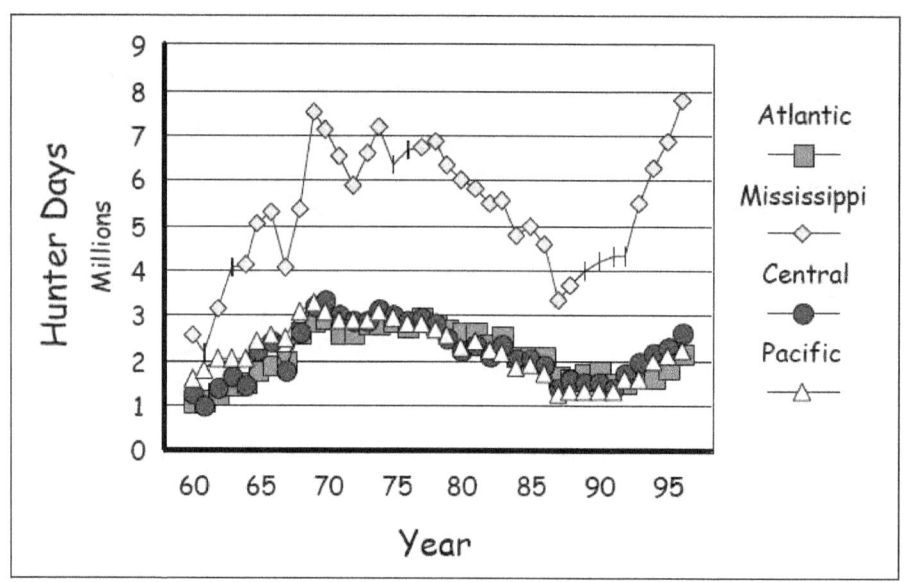

Figure 17. Estimated total U.S. waterfowl hunter days expended in the Flyways, 1961 through 1996. Pacific Flyway data since 1965 include estimates for Alaska. Data from P. Padding (USFWS, MBMO), (personal communication).

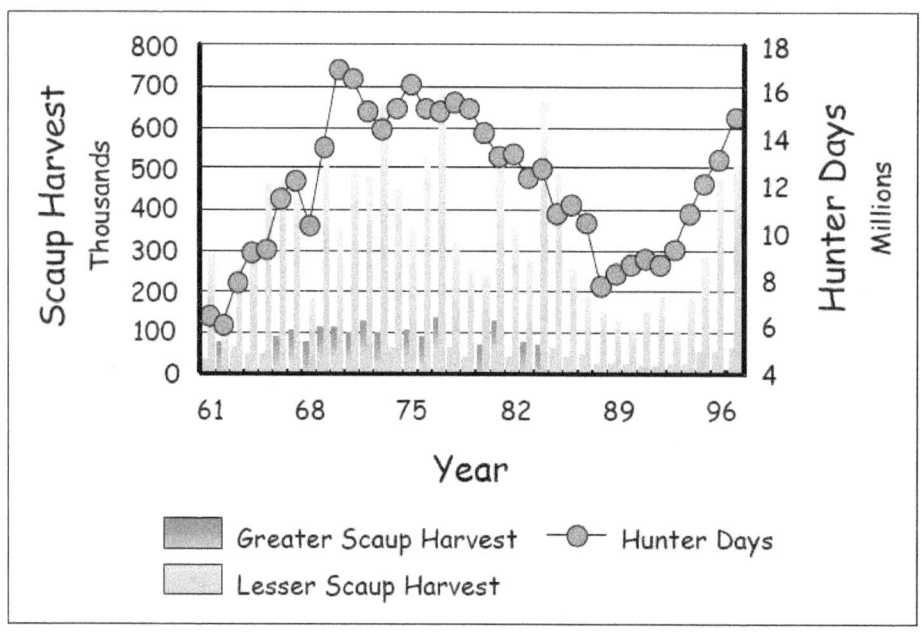

Figure 18. Total U.S. harvest of greater and lesser scaup (bars) and total estimated hunter days (dots) for all Flyways, 1961 through 1996. Data from P. Padding (USFWS, MBMO), (personal communication).

Harvest and Age Ratios in Canada

Harvests of both greater and lesser scaup in Canada (Table 8, Figures 19 and 20) have declined since 1974 (P<0.001 for both species). Age ratios for greater scaup in the Canadian harvests have varied from 1.13 immatures/adult in 1978 to 4.44 immatures/adult in 1973, but no trend was evident (P= 0.65). Age ratios of lesser scaup in the harvest in Canada also varied greatly (range=1.7–4.5), and no trend was evident during 1969–1997. However, when the substantial change in 1997 was excluded, there was a decline in the ratio (P=0.01, ≈1.5% per year).

Harvest in the United States and Canada

The harvests of greater scaup and lesser scaup in the U.S. and Canada combined have declined since 1974 (P<0.001 and P=0.01, respectively, Table 9, Figures 21 and 22). We detected no trend in the proportion of the total harvest taken in the U.S. during 1974–1997 (P=0.203 for greater scaup, P=0.520 for lesser scaup, Figures 23 and 24).

MIDWINTER SURVEYS

Estimates of scaup from the Midwinter Survey declined during 1955–1997 (P<0.001, Table 10, Figure 25). Declines in the Atlantic and Mississippi Flyways accounted for much of the overall change (P=0.004 in the Atlantic Flyway, P=0.008 in the Mississippi Flyway).

CHRISTMAS BIRD COUNTS

CBC data show that from 1955 through 1995, greater scaup declined 3.2% per year (P<0.01, n=902) (Table 11). Greater scaup declined over the entire CBC area from 1955 through 1987 (3.9% per year, P<0.01, n=752). Since 1988, greater scaup totals have been stable, with the exception of an increase in the Atlantic Flyway (8.7% per year, P=0.04, n=249).

Counts from 1955 through 1995 revealed no trend in numbers of lesser scaup (P=0.26, n=1506). Lesser scaup declined around the Great Lakes from 1955 through 1987, but their numbers did not change in other areas or across the CBC survey area during 1988–1995.

All scaup declined 4.8% per year in the Great Lakes region from 1955 through 1987 (P<0.01, 229 counts), and 3.5% per year for the entire CBC period. From 1988 through 1995, the population on the Great Lakes increased about 16.0% per year (P=0.04, n=172).

Table 8. Scaup harvest (1974 through 1996) and age ratios in the harvest in Canada, 1969 through 1997. NA=Not analyzed. Data from H. Lévesque (CWS), (personal communications).

Hunting season	Greater scaup		Lesser scaup		Total scaup
	Harvest	Immatures per adult ratio	Harvest	Immatures per adult ratio	
1969	NA[1]	2.86	NA	4.48	NA
1970	NA	3.30	NA	3.83	NA
1971	NA	2.19	NA	3.26	NA
1972	NA	2.69	NA	2.04	NA
1973	NA	4.44	NA	4.26	NA
1974	44,768	2.03	108,728	3.75	152,271
1975	70,996	1.19	136,472	3.58	207,468
1976	75,539	3.33	148,111	2.89	223,650
1977	71,499	2.91	114,325	2.50	185,701
1978	42,709	1.13	96,029	1.68	138,738
1979	50,443	2.71	99,122	2.39	149,565
1980	54,237	2.68	137,050	3.39	191,287
1981	49,672	3.21	126,391	3.24	176,063
1982	34,239	1.63	108,086	2.17	142,325
1983	55,285	2.91	101,334	2.50	156,619
1984	48,376	2.09	109,916	3.42	158,292
1985	51,109	2.80	115,994	2.81	167,106
1986	53,573	2.41	101,932	2.26	155,505
1987	24,337	2.14	72,417	3.31	96,754
1988	32,419	1.40	73,151	3.14	105,570
1989	33,865	1.76	86,000	2.76	119,865
1990	27,694	1.90	68,364	2.31	96,058
1991	19,693	3.26	66,833	2.35	91,526
1992	18,191	2.14	53,135	1.89	80,906
1993	25,082	2.98	69,986	2.50	90,365
1994	17,725	2.90	58,677	3.59	73,604
1995	20,358	3.22	56,850	2.32	77,208
1996	16,422	1.94	41,435	1.69	57,856
1997	12,963	1.79	43,941	4.77	44,944

[1] No harvest data prior to 1974.

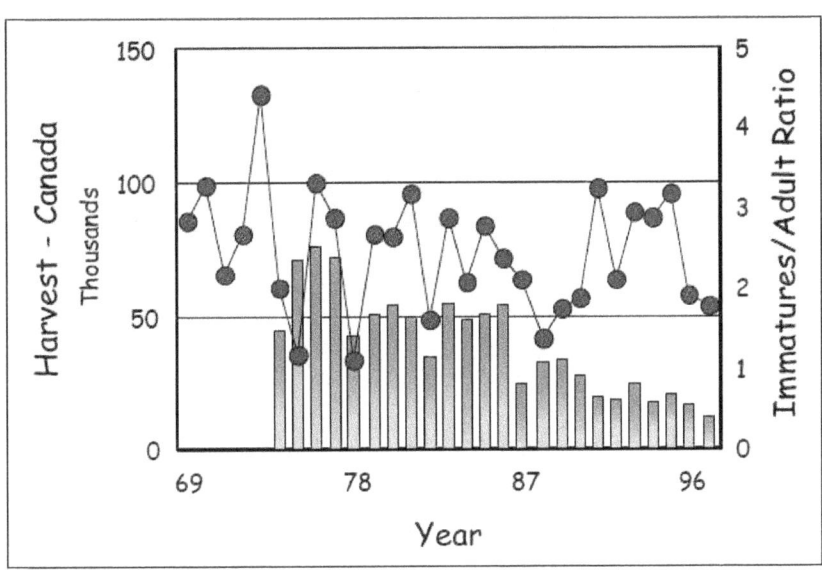

Figure 19. Greater scaup harvest in Canada, 1973 through 1997 (bars) and immatures/adult age ratios in the harvest, 1969 through 1997 (dots). Data from H. Lévesque (CWS), (personal communications).

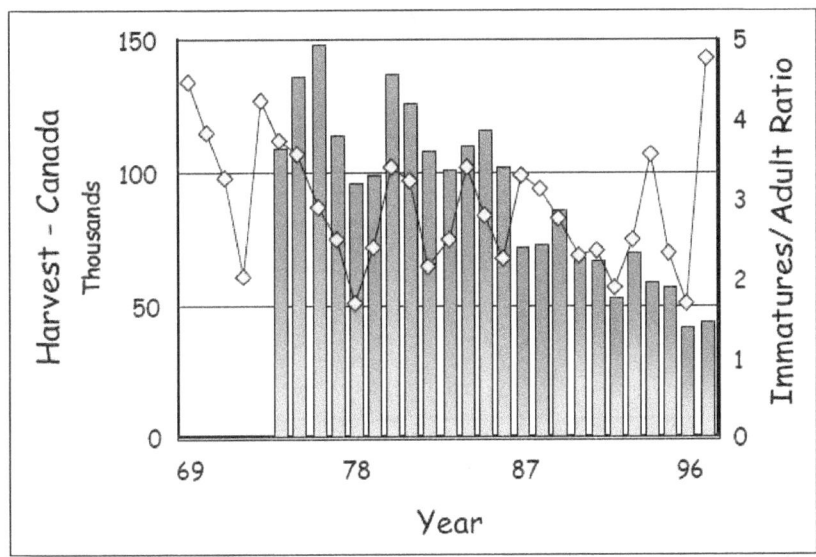

Figure 20. Lesser scaup harvest in Canada, 1973 through 1997 (bars) and immatures/adult age ratios in the harvest, 1969 through 1997 (diamonds). Data from H. Lévesque (CWS), (personal communications).

Table 9. Combined U.S. and Canadian greater and lesser scaup harvest, 1974–1997.

Hunting season	Harvest		
	Greater scaup	Lesser scaup	Total scaup
1974	110,568	558,203	668,771
1975	173,796	495,572	669,368
1976	164,439	683,111	847,550
1977	204,113	800,888	1,005,001
1978	103,709	412,929	516,638
1979	91,143	353,222	444,365
1980	122,737	376,950	499,687
1981	175,372	676,391	851,763
1982	75,139	466,886	542,025
1983	130,285	374,034	504,319
1984	120,576	773,216	893,792
1985	116,709	604,297	721,006
1986	91,673	352,032	443,705
1987	70,237	259,417	329,654
1988	58,819	221,651	280,470
1989	60,265	213,800	274,065
1990	55,494	171,564	227,058
1991	38,793	224,333	263,126
1992	48,840	241,466	290,306
1993	50,608	174,457	225,065
1994	46,070	235,734	281,804
1995	74,258	342,750	417,008
1996	69,021	514,635	583,656
1997	74,494	545,150	619,644

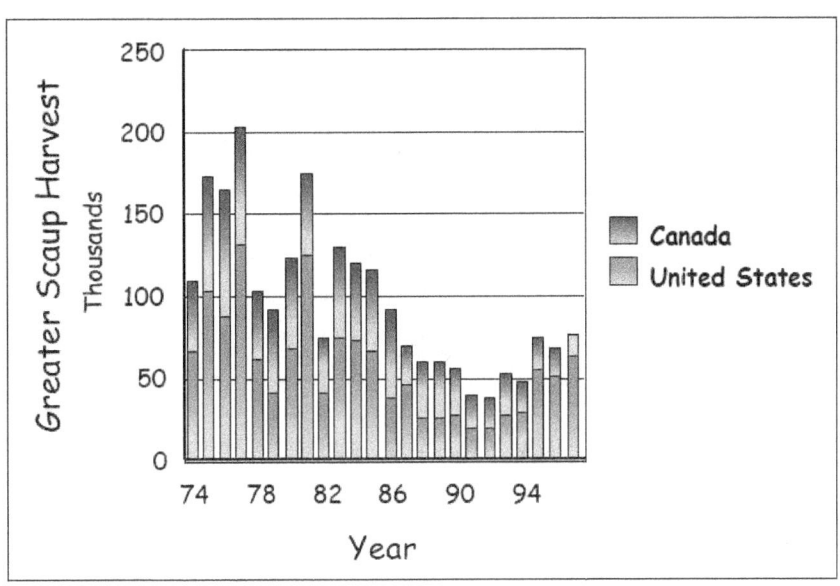

Figure 21. Total greater scaup harvest in Canada and the U.S., 1974–1997.

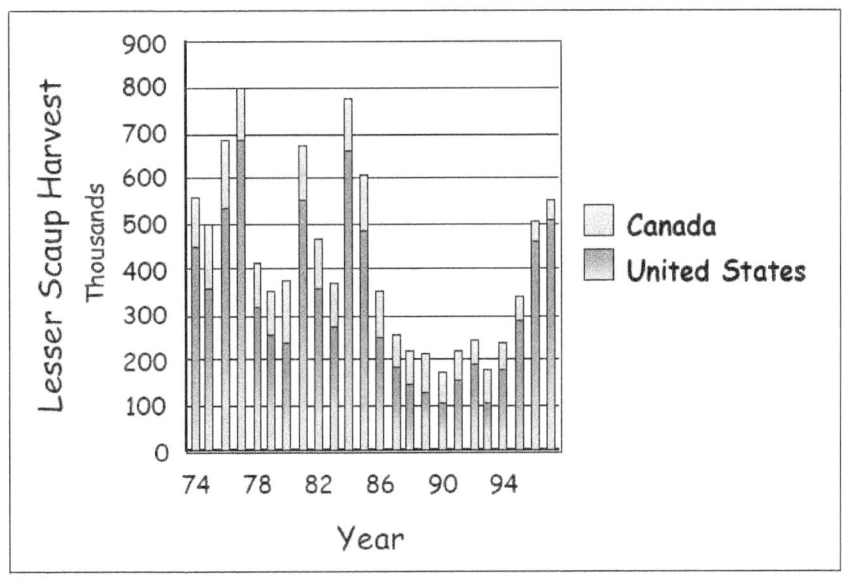

Figure 22. Total lesser scaup harvest in Canada and the U.S., 1974–1997.

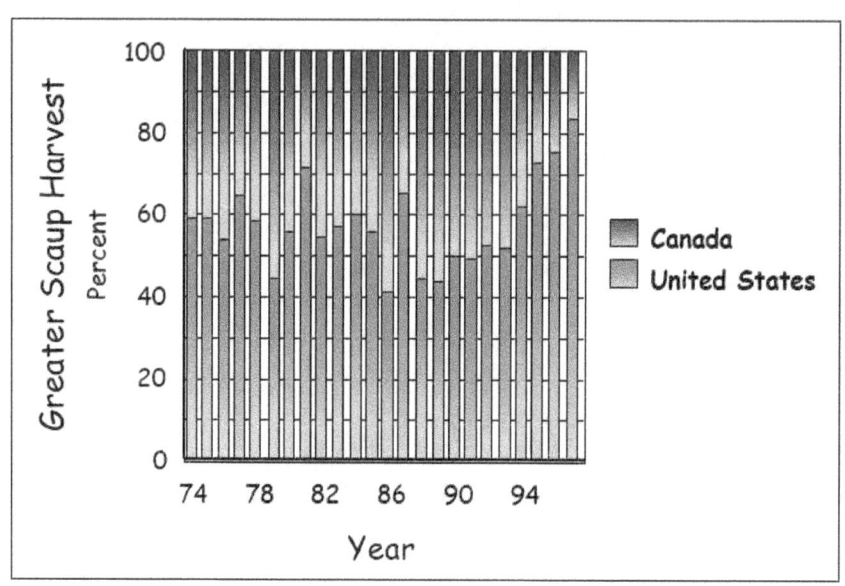

Figure 23. Proportions of greater scaup harvest occurring in Canada and the U.S., 1974–1997.

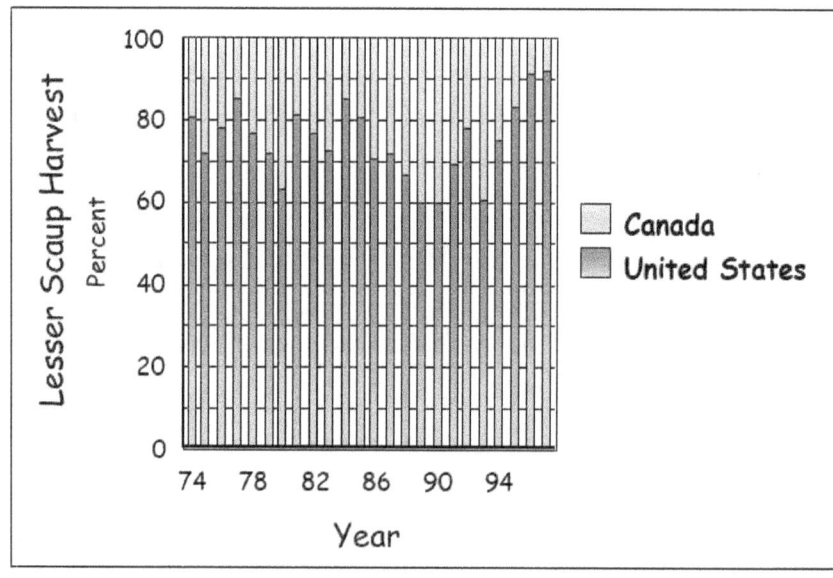

Figure 24. Proportions of lesser scaup harvest occurring in Canada and the U.S., 1974–1997.

Table 10. Midwinter Survey counts of scaup in the Flyways, 1955–1997. Scaup counted in Mexico in 1978 through 1982 and in 1985, 1988, 1991, 1994, and 1997 are included in the Central and Pacific Flyway totals. Data from Benning (1997), Conant and Voelzer (1997), Ferguson et al. (1997), Serie and Cruz (1997), Sharp (1997), and K. Gamble and B. Trost (USFWS, MBMO), (personal communications). NS=Not surveyed.

Year	Count				
	Flyway				Total
	Atlantic	Mississippi	Central	Pacific	
1955	888,003	246,601	26,654	241,833	1,403,091
1956	824,318	144,966	60,881	20,426	1,050,591
1957	603,639	258,240	84,333	175,122	1,121,334
1958	588,878	223,911	548,549	339,608	1,700,946
1959	563,018	283,138	559,840	410,043	1,816,039
1960	619,200	965,030	35,394	182,882	1,802,506
1961	699,700	1,610,508	13,887	194,708	2,518,803
1962	706,600	1,755,382	53,340	279,132	2,794,454
1963	610,000	1,675,102	237,729	434,328	2,957,159
1964	856,900	752,086	36,581	280,423	1,925,990
1965	694,300	402,470	72,022	273,817	1,442,609
1966	926,700	309,832	36,889	156,501	1,429,922
1967	570,200	289,685	32,316	104,099	996,300
1968	526,000	785,800	57,335	183,486	1,552,621
1969	743,300	1,421,400	42,669	116,752	2,324,121
1970	396,500	1,043,900	63,445	93,784	1,597,629
1971	686,200	958,600	34,959	102,799	1,782,558
1972	429,100	181,700	48,305	135,081	794,186
1973	400,998	963,600	58,835	148,135	1,571,568
1974	452,978	725,600	60,911	87,931	1,327,420
1975	609,084	230,800	190,825	230,925	1,261,634

Table 10 (continued). Midwinter Survey counts of scaup in the Flyways, 1955–1997. Scaup counted in surveys in Mexico in 1978 through 1982 and in 1985, 1988, 1991, 1994, and 1997 are included in the Central and Pacific Flyway totals. Data from Benning (1997), Conant and Voelzer (1997), Ferguson et al. (1997), Serie and Cruz (1997), Sharp (1997), and K. Gamble and B. Trost (USFWS, MBMO), (personal communications).

Year			Count						Total
					Flyway				
				Central			Pacific		
	Atlantic	Mississippi	Central	Mexico – Central	Central Total	Pacific	Mexico – Pacific	Pacific Total	
1976	300,731	658,300	169,060	NS	169,060	213,612	NS	213,612	1,341,703
1977	437,763	624,700	63,794	NS	63,794	222,651	NS	222,651	1,348,908
1978	290,848	169,000	52,960	207,114	260,074	245,484	60,976	306,460	1,026,382
1979	387,189	947,000	29,348	157,828	187,176	181,778	70,120	251,898	1,515,967
1980	409,694	368,000	74,001	75,055	149,056	186,790	51,520	238,310	964,484
1981	324,828	346,300	62,767	216,490	279,257	169,854	64,030	233,884	840,982
1982	449,088	573,100	140,349	148,385	288,734	146,418	66,920	213,338	1,168,606
1983	373,566	173,100	38,149	NS	38,149	136,203	NS	136,203	682,869
1984	379,071	332,000	61,260	NS	61,260	214,583	NS	214,583	925,654
1985	311,688	673,400	75,800	57,870	133,670	207,501	53,100	260,601	1,192,589
1986	411,017	351,100	116,200	NS	116,200	223,838	NS	223,838	98,5955
1987	341,125	453,200	59,157	NS	59,157	87,214	NS	87,214	88,1539
1988	258,682	499,500	79,639	35,605	115,244	185,045	59,200	244,245	94,3227
1989	377,683	742,100	19,351	NS	19,351	143,363	NS	143,363	1,263,146
1990	465,045	350,498	36,683	NS	36,683	196,652	NS	196,652	1,012,195
1991	675,837	106,388	12,667	87,835	100,502	302,177	100,500	402,677	1,084,402
1992	462,910	411,620	24,737	NS	24,737	170,566	NS	170,566	1,045,096
1993	649,605	27,395	57,012	NS	57,012	137,225	NS	137,225	814,225
1994	714,634	124,780	92,990	64,450	157,440	205,216	50,900	256,116	1,044,630
1995	1,143,582	103,490	51,886	NS	51,886	129,188	NS	129,188	1,376,260
1996	404,796	363,208	76,855	NS	76,855	87,099	NS	87,099	855,103
1997	361,953	55,938	55,550	8972	64,522	213,810	59,600	273,410	631,701

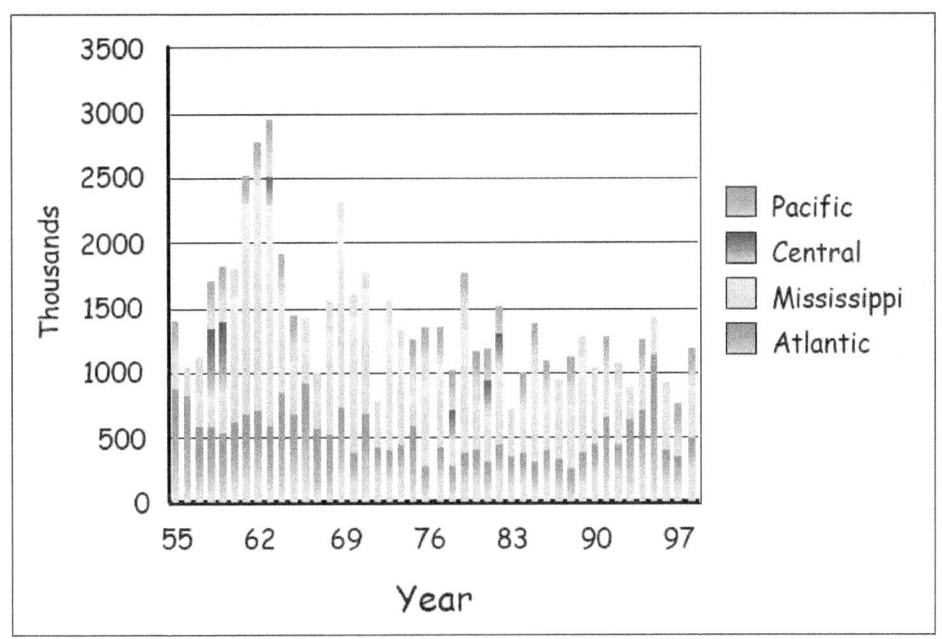

Figure 25. Total scaup counts in the Flyways from the Midwinter Inventories, 1955–1997.
Scaup counted in surveys in Mexico in 1978 through 1982 and in 1985, 1988, 1991, 1994,
and 1997 are included in the Central and Pacific Flyway totals. Data from Benning (1997),
Conant and Voelzer (1997), Ferguson et al. (1997), Serie and Cruz (1997), Sharp (1997), and
K. Gamble and B. Trost (USFWS, MBMO), (personal communications).

Table 11. Population trends for greater and lesser scaup, as indicated by Christmas Bird Counts. Data from J. Sauer (USGS BRD), (personal communication).

	Time period									
	1955–1995				1955–1987			1988–1995		
Region	Trend[1]	P	n	95% CI	Trend	P	n	Trend	P	n
All scaup										
Survey–Wide	−4.4	0.20	1621	−11.0 to 2.3	−1.0	0.21	1444	−2.4	0.15	1071
Atlantic Flyway	−8.80	0.22	590	−22.7 to −5.2	−1.6	0.23	529	−2.7	0.53	388
Great Lakes	−3.5	<0.01	258	−5.3 to −1.7	−4.8	<0.01	229	16.0	0.04	172
Western Gulf of Mexico	−1.8	0.20	80	−4.5 to −0.9	−1.9	0.22	68	−6.1	0.26	49
Pacific Coast	−0.3	0.77	244	−2.2 to −1.6	−0.2	0.89	214	−2.6	0.23	181
Greater scaup										
Survey–Wide	−3.2	<0.01	902	−4.5 to −1.9	−3.9	<0.01	752	0.3	0.90	559
Atlantic Flyway	−4.2	<0.01	404	−5.6 to −2.9	−4.5	<0.01	354	8.7	0.04	249
Great Lakes	−3.5	<0.01	170	−5.9 to −1.2	−4.5	<0.01	151	18.0	0.07	105
Western Gulf of Mexico	2.8	0.22	59	−1.6 to 7.3	2.1	0.30	48	−0.5	0.97	30
Pacific Coast	−2.4	0.10	185	−5.2 to 0.4	−3.6	0.03	155	−3.2	0.17	134
Lesser scaup										
Survey–Wide	−4.0	0.26	1506	−11.0 to 3.0	−0.3	0.76	1338	−2.8	0.26	984
Atlantic Flyway	−7.0	0.31	511	−20.5 to 6.6	0.0	0.99	452	−5.3	0.31	332
Great Lakes	−1.8	0.31	232	−5.4 to 1.7	−5.1	0.01	202	17.1	0.07	150
Western Gulf of Mexico	−2.3	0.10	79	−5.0 to 0.4	−2.5	0.11	67	−5.3	0.36	49
Pacific Coast	−1.5	0.12	230	−3.3 to 0.4	−0.2	0.88	203	−3.7	0.19	172

[1] Percent change per year.

MODELING POPULATION DYNAMICS OF LESSER SCAUP

We developed and compared mathematical models of lesser scaup population dynamics to better understand factors affecting the size of the population and to aid harvest management. To develop the models we used annual measures of spring population size, recruitment (age ratios in the U.S. harvest), wetland abundance in the pothole region of the U.S. and Canada, and U.S. harvest during 1961–1998. We assessed two forms of models: one set on an original scale which allowed for arithmetic relationships among estimates, and the other set on a logarithmic scale which allowed for multiplicative relationships among estimates. For both the arithmetic and multiplicative model forms, we began with models that included all parameters, and sequentially eliminated them; for each reduction we compared performance of the models with a small sample version of Akaike's Information Criteria (AIC, Hurvich and Tsai 1991). We also compared how well each model fit the data using AIC (Burnham and Anderson 1998).

Our initial analyses of the effects of special seasons and bag limits revealed no evidence that they affected population trends. However, a consistent downward trend in the lesser scaup population began in 1983. Therefore, after evaluating models for the full set of years, 1961–1998, we assessed models for the period 1983–1998.

Both model forms used indices of population, harvest, and recruitment. Estimates of the size of the lesser scaup population were derived from strata 1–50 (excluding the tundra strata 8, 9, 10, 11, and 13) of the Spring Survey (Smith 1995). U.S. harvest and harvest age ratio estimates were produced from results of hunter surveys; so those estimates were not fully independent (Martin and Carney 1977). We considered using similar estimates from Canada, but did not because estimates for Canada are available only since 1974 and because most of the lesser scaup harvest in North America occurs in the U.S. Our index to recruitment was the age ratio in the harvest, after adjusting for relative vulnerability of immatures to adults (Reynolds 1987). Unfortunately, banding data were insufficient to derive annual estimates of relative vulnerability. Therefore, we used a constant relative vulnerability rate of 3.06 derived for 1959–1966, when at least 100 individuals of each age and sex class were banded during late summer. Finally, we assessed the value of including estimates of wetland numbers from Canada (strata 26–40) and the U.S. (strata 41–49) as possible determinants of recruitment.

MODELS
Arithmetic Models

Variables in our arithmetic models (number of scaup in the population, number harvested, number recruited, etc.) were on the original scale. Conceptually, the full arithmetic model explained the size of the population in the next time step as the current population multiplied by the estimated survival rate of ducks during the non-hunting season, the addition of young recruited, and the subtraction of scaup harvested in the U.S.:

$$\begin{pmatrix} Spring \\ population \end{pmatrix}_{t+1} = \begin{pmatrix} Non\text{-}hunting \\ season \\ survival\ rate \end{pmatrix}\begin{pmatrix} Spring \\ population \end{pmatrix}_{t} + (Recruitment)_t - (Harvest)_t + (Error$$

We estimated our conceptual model as a regression equation:

$$: c + \phi b_t + (\beta_r r_t + \beta_{Canada} Ponds_t^{Canada} + \beta_{U.S.} Ponds_t^{U.S.}) + \beta_h h_t + u_t + e_t$$

In the fully parameterized regression equation, b = spring population, ϕ = survival rate during the non-hunting season, $\beta r + \beta_{Canada} Ponds^{Canada} + \beta_{U.S.} Ponds^{U.S.}$ represents recruitment, h = U.S. harvest, u = model error, and e = sampling error. The survival rate during the non-hunting season, ϕ, was estimated by regression. It conceptually accounted for all natural mortality of fledged young and adults, crippling loss in the U.S., and hunting mortality in Canada. The recruitment term contains three explanatory variables: (1) recruitment estimate, (2) wetland numbers in the U.S., and (3) wetland numbers in Canada. The number of young recruited to the fall population was estimated by the ratio of young to adults in the fall harvest (ar_t), corrected for different vulnerability of young and adults (rv). This corrected age ratio was multiplied by the spring population estimate.

$$r_t = b_t \frac{ar_t}{rv}.$$

Regression estimates of the effects of wetland numbers on population size were also included, and the net effect was that estimates of recruitment were a compromise between our direct estimate, r_t, and the regression on wetland numbers. Our estimates of recruitment were not independent from estimates of the spring population size. The spring population plus recruitment summed to the fall population before any harvest.

We included coefficients on the recruitment and harvest terms for two reasons. First, they scale the recruitment and harvest estimates to the spring population estimates. The differences in scale were a form of systematic measurement error called .proportional bias.. The coefficients on the recruitment and harvest terms also were confounded with the estimates of survival during the non-hunting season. Because ϕ was a coefficient of only the spring population term, harvest and recruitment were confounded with non-hunting season mortality.

We included a constant in equation (1) to account for any constant differences between the spring population estimates and the harvest and recruitment estimates. This constant difference is another form of systematic measurement error called .level bias..

We included separate terms for model error and survey sample error and assumed that these were independent. The survey sample error term accounts only for sampling error in the spring population estimates. Estimates of sampling error were not available for harvest or age ratios (Geissler 1990). We accounted for sampling error for harvest and recruitment with the model error term. That should not be problematic if the survey sample errors of those estimates were relatively constant. We assumed that model error was constant.

Because the direct estimates of the survey sample variances were highly variable, we fit a generalized variance function (GVF) relating the mean to the variance to obtain more stable estimates. We modeled several functions of the variance:

$$Var(e_t) = \gamma_0 + \tau_t + \gamma_1 b_t + \gamma_2 b_t^2 ,$$
$$Var(e_t) = \gamma_0 + \tau_t + \gamma_1 b_t ,$$
$$Var(e_t) = \gamma_0 + \tau_t + \gamma_2 b_t^2 . \qquad (2)$$

The relative variances decreased over time, possibly due to improvements in the Spring Survey. Temporal changes in variances were accounted for through the variable T_t. We used AIC to choose between the GVFs then used the predictions for the variances of e_t in the regression model (1).

The errors of the original population data were not constant, but the relative errors of the log transformations, $\mathrm{Var}(b_{t+1})/\mathrm{Mean}(b_{t+1})^2$ were constant. We verified this by examining the plot of the population estimates and variances from the Spring Survey (Figure 26). This supported use of the multiplicative model form.

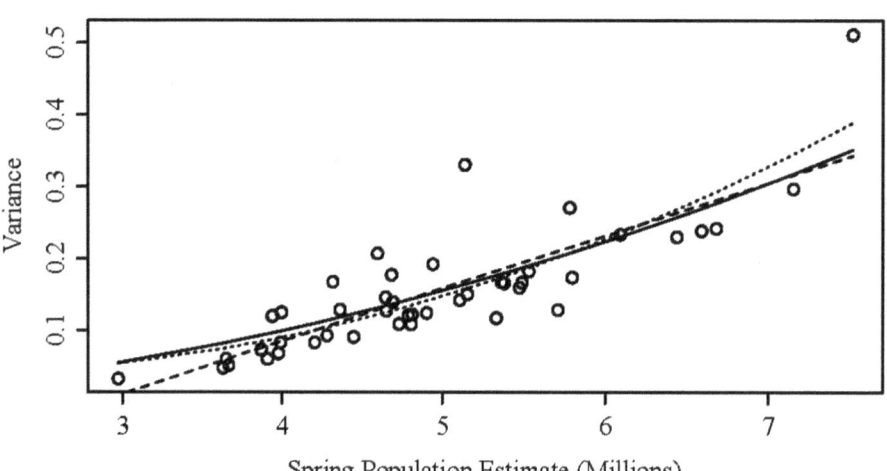

Figure 26. Spring population estimates (circles) of lesser scaup and their associated estimates of variance, 1961–1998. The solid line is the favored Generalized Variance Function (GVF) which includes only the quadratic term. The dotted line is the full GVF with constant, linear and quadratic terms; the dashed line is a reduced GVF with only a linear term and no constant.

We checked for correlations over time by examining sample autocorrelations, then fitting Box–Jenkins ARIMA models (Box and Jenkins 1976) where necessary.

Multiplicative Models

We believed that it was more realistic and statistically appropriate to model the dynamics of lesser scaup populations by multiplying rates (e.g., survival rate, recruitment rate, etc.) with a population estimate, rather than summing estimates (as was done in the arithmetic models). Whereas our arithmetic models added and subtracted terms on the original scale, our multiplicative models added and subtracted logs of rates, which was equivalent to multiplying untransformed (original scale) terms. Using logs allowed us to assume that the survey sample error was constant. Our fully parameterized multiplicative model was:

$$\begin{pmatrix} Spring \\ population \end{pmatrix}_{t+1} = \begin{pmatrix} Non-hunting \\ season \\ survival\ rate \end{pmatrix} \begin{pmatrix} Spring \\ population \end{pmatrix}_t \begin{pmatrix} Hunting \\ season \\ survival\ rate \end{pmatrix} \begin{pmatrix} Recruitment \\ rate \end{pmatrix} (Error$$

$$\log(b_{t+1}) = \log(\phi) + \beta_b \log(b_t) + \beta_{hs}\log(hs_t) + \beta_{rr}\log(rr_t) +$$
$$\beta_{Canada}\log(Ponds_t^{Canada}) + \beta_{U.S.}\log(Ponds_t^{U.S.}) + u_t + e_t \ .$$

Again, our conceptual model is estimated as a regression.

The recruitment rate, rr, was the estimated rate at which young were recruited to the fall population relative to the number of adults present:

$$rr_t = 1 + \frac{ar_t}{rv}$$

The estimate of hunting season survival rate was calculated from estimates of harvest, recruitment, and population size:

$$hs_t = 1 - hr_t, \qquad (3)$$

$$hr_t = \frac{\cdot\cdot_t}{h\cdot rr_\cdot} \ .$$

Estimates of U.S. and Canadian wetland numbers were used as additional determinants of recruitment. The rate at which young were recruited can be estimated by summing the terms for recruitment rate and wetland numbers.

On the log scale, the non-hunting season survival was a constant, $\log(\phi)$, and not a coefficient of the spring population as in the arithmetic models. The regression coefficients for recruitment rate, β_{rr}, and hunting season survival, β_{hs}, were not confounded by the non-hunting season survival, as in the arithmetic models. However, these coefficients were still used to put recruitment and harvest estimates on the same scale as the spring population estimates.

On the log scale, both the model and survey errors were assumed to be constant. The mean of the relative survey sample variances became the estimate for the survey sample errors.

We initially assessed multiplicative models for the entire period, 1961–1998. Upon review of these results, we repeated the modeling procedure for the more recent period, 1983–1998. Our goal was to find what factors significantly determined change in the spring population from year to year and to obtain estimates of the spring population apart from the sampling error. These estimates were weighted averages of the spring population survey estimates and the model predictions. The weights were a function of the survey sample and model variances.

MODELING RESULTS

We found no significant autocorrelations of the errors in any of the arithmetic or multiplicative models. This was probably due to the short length of the series or the models accounting for the time series variation.

We fit linear and quadratic terms for the GVFs. All models included a linear decrease over time. We preferred equation (2), which had the lowest AIC and appeared to describe the relationship reasonably well (Figure 27). The coefficient, γ, was estimated at 0.0072 (se=0.00119). The constant was 2.8×10^{12} (se=1.5×10^{12}), and the time trend was -1.5×10^{9} (se=7.4×10^{8}). For the multiplicative model, the predicted GVFs were divided by the square of the spring population estimates.

According to AIC statistics, the best model for the entire period, 1961–1998, described population size as a function of the size of the previous population:

$$\log(b_{t+1}) = \log(b_t) + u_t + e_t .$$

The standard error of the model, u_t, was 0.0083. The next best model for this period included a term for the non-hunting season survival rate; this was estimated as 0.99 and was not different (P>0.1) from 1.0. Our final model did not include this term, which was equivalent to forcing this parameter to equal 1.0. This parameter accounted for not only non-hunting season survival in this model but also recruitment, harvest, and any level biases of these estimates. Including recruitment and survival during the hunting season did not improve model performance. In fact, the estimated coefficient for the recruitment term was non-significantly (P>0.1) negative; negative recruitment was counterintuitive.

The best model for the period 1983–1998 described population size as a function of the previous population size, and survival rate during hunting:

$$\log(b_{t+1}) \ = \ \log(b_t) \ + \ \beta_{hs}\log(hs_t) \ + \ u_t \ + \ e_t \ .$$

The estimate of β_{hs} (1.1, se=0.19) was not significantly different (P>0.1) from 1, indicating little proportional bias in this estimate. The parameter for survival rate outside the hunting season was not retained in the model, suggesting that this estimate was close to 1. The coefficient for the population size term, β_b, was estimated at 1.003, not significantly different (P>0.1) from 1. Therefore, we removed this term from the model, which was equivalent to forcing it to equal 1. The net effect was to ignore a very small rate of growth (0.3% per year) that is suggested in the absence of harvest in the U.S. Overall, the standard error of the best model was 0.0018. This model fit the data six times as well as the model from 1983–1998 that described population size only as a function of the previous population. Thirteen of 15 population estimates were within the 95% confidence interval of predictions derived from the model (Figure 27).

1961–1998 Multiplicative Model

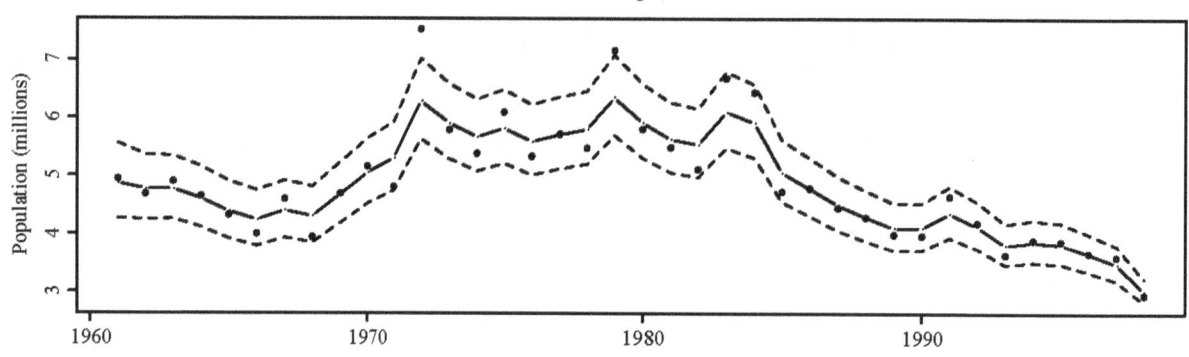

1983–1998 Multiplicative Model

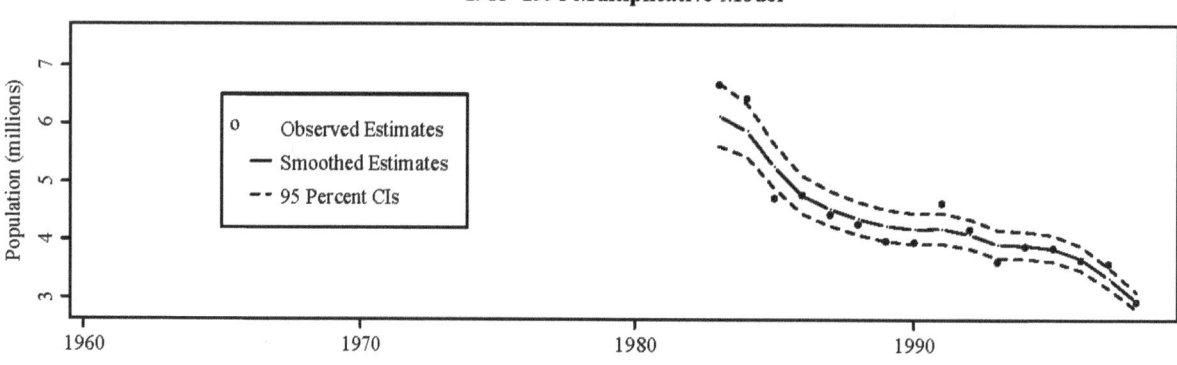

o   Observed Estimates
—   Smoothed Estimates
- -   95 Percent CIs

1983–1998 Arithmetic Model

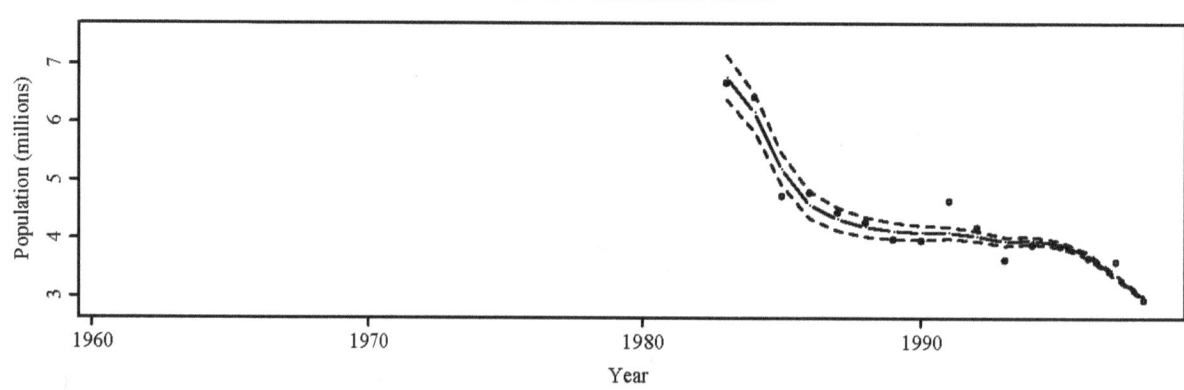

Year

Figure 27. Observed population estimates of lesser scaup and smoothed estimates that are weighted averages of the regression prediction and the observed estimate.

The best arithmetic model described population size during 1983–1998 as a function of a constant (intercept), the previous population size, and U.S. harvest:

$$b_{t+1} = c + \phi b_t + \beta_h h_t + u_t + e_t .$$

The parameter estimates for this model were: c, 743,863 (se=56,697); ϕ, 0.85 (se=0.007); β, −1.2 (se=0.22); and se of u was 0.0069. Similar to the best multiplicative model for this period, no recruitment parameters were retained in the best arithmetic model. Five of the 15 population estimates were outside the range of the 95% confidence interval for this model (Figure 27). Overall, this model did not describe variation in population size during 1983–1998 as well as the best multiplicative model. The smoothed variances of the arithmetic model appeared unrealistically small.

DISCUSSION

We believe that the most reliable measure of the size of the greater scaup population is the spring population estimate from tundra areas of Alaska and the Northwest Territories. No population trend was apparent with this index, but CBCs indicate a long-term decline across North America. There is evidence of regional variation in population trends (CBCs and J. Barclay, personal communication), but overall we consider the status of greater scaup to be stable. Termination of special scaup hunting opportunities in 1988 coincided with reduced harvest of greater scaup and improvements in spring population and CBC trends. Much of the special scaup season harvest was composed of greater scaup, but this still comprised a small portion of the total scaup harvest (Office of Migratory Bird Management 1990). We can not conclude how much, if any, of the improvements to the status of greater scaup is attributable to elimination of special scaup hunting opportunities.

Most measures of the size of the lesser scaup population indicate a long-term decline. This decline is coincident with a long-term decline in one index to recruitment. Although we were unable to demonstrate a relationship between this recruitment index and subsequent population size, we believe that the long-term deterioration in recruitment has contributed to declines in number of lesser scaup. Elimination of special scaup hunting opportunity in 1988 was not coincident with reductions in harvest of lesser scaup or an increase in the size of the spring population. In fact, the spring population estimates began declining at a significant rate in 1988. The special harvest opportunities offered prior to 1988 appeared to account for only a small part of the overall harvest of lesser scaup in the U.S. (Office of Migratory Bird

Management 1990). Lesser scaup harvest appears to have responded more to season lengths and bag limits of the regular duck season.

Our population models of lesser scaup yielded different inferences on the effects of hunting depending on the time period assessed. The size of the spring population during 1961–1998 was best described as a function of the previous population size. However, when we analyzed data from a more recent period, 1983–1998, population size was best described as a function of previous population size and harvest. In this model, increased harvest is expected to produce smaller subsequent populations. Clearly, the results of our modeling are time-dependent and this is not preferred, because it is unclear what factors will continue to influence population size in the future. However, we believe that results from the most recent period are more likely to be representative of the population dynamics of lesser scaup in the next few years. Our choice for time periods to analyze entailed several considerations. Initially, we included all years that were practical, 1961–1998. Noting the change in population trends that occurred in about 1983, we chose to evaluate models from the more recent period. We chose to not persist with our evaluation of the potential effects of eliminating special hunting opportunities (1988–1998) because this did not appear to coincide with changes in harvest or population size.

The negative effect of harvest on population size is consistent with life history characteristics of scaup. Compared to most other duck species, scaup are considered K-strategists with high annual survivorship and low reproductive potential (Patterson 1979). This provides them with limited capacity to compensate for hunting mortality through increased recruitment or increased survival outside of the hunting season (Patterson 1979, Nichols et al. 1984).

Surprisingly, our indices to recruitment (age ratio of the harvest in the U.S., or number of wetlands in the prairie potholes of the U.S. or Canada) were not retained as important parameters in any of the three best models (two from 1983–1998 and one from 1961–1998). In fact, there was a negative but nonsignificant relationship between age ratio in the U.S. harvest and subsequent population size (Table 12). This counterintuitive relationship could be related to changes in the relative vulnerability of immature scaup compared to adults. Unfortunately, banding data were insufficient to assess this question. The number of wetlands in Canada was positively related to subsequent population size, but this parameter was not retained in the final models. Wetland numbers from the pothole region may not be a particularly useful index to recruitment because most lesser scaup nest north of there.

We suggest that managers of scaup consider our population models when developing hunting regulations. Managers should also consider the quality of the data that were used to develop these models, and their potential predictive errors. Additional concerns for managers should be the relatively small number of greater scaup in North America, and the paucity of information on the trends and dynamics of this population.

The modeling reflects the types and quality of data available, assumptions we were compelled to make, and the time periods we analyzed. The lesser scaup population declined most years during 1983–1998, and so our models from this period reflect this by allowing little or no potential for population growth. The data available on lesser scaup suffer from at least three limitations. First, population estimates of lesser scaup may be inaccurate due to the similar appearance and overlapping range of greater scaup. Second, estimates of harvest and recruitment are not independent. Lastly, reliable estimates of survival are not available. Despite these limitations, we believe that our modeling provided useful insights.

The differences between our best models for 1983–1998 and 1961–1998 suggest changes in the dynamics of lesser scaup populations. The models suggest that since 1983 harvest had a negative effect on subsequent populations. Prior to then, other factors may have compensated for the effects of harvest. Another possible explanation is that biases in our data (e.g., population size, harvest, recruitment, etc.) may have systematically changed over time and these changes may have masked our ability to understand factors important to scaup population dynamics. Population estimates of scaup from Alaska prior to 1977 may be biased low (Hodges et al. 1996), but we believe that to be the only source of bias that changed prior to 1983, and we do not believe it significantly affected our results.

Table 12. Models assessed for describing changes in the size of lesser scaup populations, 1961–1997.

Period	Model parameters[1]	AIC statistic
1983–1997 Arithmetic Model	c, ϕ, h, Ponds^{Canada}, r, Ponds$^{U.S.}$	450.6
	c, ϕ, h, Ponds^{Canada}, r	443.2
	c, ϕ, h, Ponds^{Canada}	437.5
	c, ϕ, h	435.3
	c, ϕ	438.2
1961–1997 Multiplicative Model	b^f, ϕ, hs, rr	−17.6
	b^f, ϕ, hs	−22.4
	b^f, ϕ	−27.1
	b^f	−34.3
1983–1997 Multiplicative Model	b^e, hs, ϕ, Ponds^{Canada}, rr, Ponds$^{U.S.}$	450.5
	b^e, hs, ϕ, Ponds^{Canada}	437.4
	b^e, hs, ϕ	436.2
	b^e, hs	436.6
	b^f, hs	434.4
	b^f	438.0

[1] b^f=population size in previous year (coefficient of this estimate fixed at 1.0), b^e=population size in previous year (coefficient estimated by regression), ϕ=survival rate during the non-hunting season, hs=survival rate during the hunting season, rr=recruitment rate, Ponds^{Canada}=number of wetlands during spring in south-central Canada, Ponds$^{U.S.}$=number of spring wetlands in north-central U.S.

Future modeling efforts could benefit from several improvements in the data, especially independent estimates of harvest and recruitment, estimates of the standard errors of their measurements, and an understanding of changes in sampling errors of spring population estimates. Additional analysis of population estimates from Alaska might improve the accuracy of estimates prior to 1977. Lastly, a Bayesian analytical approach likely would improve our understanding of sampling errors of estimates and allow us to better account for uncertainty in the model.

INFORMATION NEEDS

After considering the available information, we believe that it is reasonable to monitor greater and lesser scaup spring populations by ascribing each species to particular survey strata. However, we recommend field investigations to verify this assumption. A procedure for determining the proportion of each species present in each breeding survey stratum is needed. Repeated regularly, the survey also could be used to monitor changes in the distribution of both species.

Movement and distribution of the two species should be assessed to determine important migration and wintering areas. Surveys on the wintering range would need modifications in order to identify the two species and provide survey coverage of offshore habitats.

A more complete understanding of scaup population dynamics would have been possible with contemporary measures of their survival rates. This assessment may be especially important because the changes in sex ratios in the harvest indicate that female survival is declining. Future research should address this information need, perhaps through radio telemetry studies.

The apparent decline in lesser scaup recruitment suggests that other concerns should be investigated. For example, cross-seasonal influences of contaminants and changing diet of scaup on the Great Lakes and along the Gulf Coast merit research, and the effects of a diet of zebra mussels on survival and recruitment should be assessed.

ACKNOWLEDGMENTS

Judy Bladen provided the information on scaup band recoveries. Jim Kelley provided computer programs and data we used in the evaluation of band returns. Hélène Lévesque provided harvest and age ratio data for Canada. Paul Padding provided U.S. harvest data and advice, and reviewed the section on harvest and age ratios in the harvest. Doug Benning, Bruce Conant, Jim Dubovsky, Ken Gamble, Jeff Peterson, Jerry Serie, Dave Sharp, and Bob Trost provided other information or advice we used in the assessment. John Sauer conducted the analyses of Christmas Bird Count data. Robert Blohm, Jerry Serie, Ken Gamble, Khristi Wilkins, Tim Moser, Ted Nichols, and Dave Sharp provided helpful reviews of drafts of this report. We also appreciate the efforts of anonymous reviewers of drafts. Figures 1 and 2 are reproduced from Bellrose (1980) with the permission of The Wildlife Management Institute.

LITERATURE CITED

Austin, J.E., C.M. Custer, and A.D. Afton. 1998. Lesser scaup (Aythya affinis). Number 338 in A. Poole and F. Gill, editors, The Birds of North America. The Birds of North America, Inc., Philadelphia, Pennsylvania.

Banks, R.C. 1986. Subspecies of the greater scaup and their names. Wilson Bulletin 98:433–444.

Barclay, J.S. and J.M. Zingo. 1993. Winter scaup populations in Connecticut coastal waters. The Connecticut Warbler 13:137–150.

Bellrose, F.C. 1980. Ducks, geese, and swans of North America. Third edition. Stackpole Books, Harrisburg, Pennsylvania

Benning, D. 1997. 1997 Mexico winter waterfowl survey of interior highlands and lower west coast. Unpublished report, U.S. Fish and Wildlife Service, Portland, Oregon.

Box, G.E.P., and G. M. Jenkins. 1976. Time series analysis: forecasting and control. Second Edition. Holden-Day, San Francisco, California.

Burnham, K.P. and D.R. Anderson. 1998. Model selection and inference. Springer, New York, New York.

Caithamer, D.F. and G. Smith. 1995. North American ducks. Pages 34–37 in E.T. LaRoe, G.S. Farris, C.E. Puckett, P.D. Doran, and M.J. Mac, editors. Our Living Resources: A Report to the Nation on the Distribution, Abundance, and Health of U.S. Plants, Animals, and Ecosystems. U.S. Department of the Interior, National Biological Service. Washington, D.C.

Canadian Wildlife Service Waterfowl Committee. 1998. Status of migratory game birds in Canada – November 2, 1998. A. Filion and K.M. Dickson, editors. Canadian Wildlife Service, Ottawa, Ontario.

Clapp, R.B., M.K. Klimkiewicz, and J.H. Kennard. 1982. Longevity records of North American birds: Gaviidae through Alcidae. Journal of Field Ornithology 53:81–124.

Conant, B. and J.F. Voelzer. 1997. Winter waterfowl survey: Mexico west coast and Baja California. Unpublished report, U.S. Fish and Wildlife Service, Portland, Oregon.

Eggeman, D.R. and F.A. Johnson. 1989. Variation in effort and methodology for the midwinter waterfowl inventory in the Atlantic Flyway. Wildlife Society Bulletin 17:227–233.

Eggeman, D.R., F.A. Johnson, M.J. Conroy, and D.H. Brakhage. 1997. Evaluation of an aerial quadrat survey for monitoring wintering duck populations. Journal of Wildlife Management 61:403–412.

Ferguson, C., J. Wortham, and R. Migoya. 1997. Winter waterfowl survey: east coast of Mexico – Rio Grande Delta to Northeastern Yucutan. Unpublished report, U.S. Fish and Wildlife Service, Portland, Oregon.

Geissler, P. H. 1990. Estimation of confidence intervals for federal waterfowl harvest surveys. Journal of Wildlife Management. 54:201–205.

Hodges, J.I., J.G. King, B. Conant, and H.A. Hanson. 1996. Aerial surveys of waterbirds in Alaska 1957–94: population trends and observer variability. Information and Technology Report 4, National Biological Service, Denver, Colorado.

Hurvich, C. M., and C. Tsai. 1991. Regression and time series model selection in small samples. Biometrika 76:297.307.

Jewel, L.L. 1913. Some North American birds in Panama. Auk 30:422–429.

Johnsgard, P.A. 1975. Waterfowl of North America. Indiana University Press, Bloomington.

Johnson, D.H. and J.W. Grier. 1988. Determinants of breeding distributions of ducks. Wildlife Monograph number 100. The Wildlife Society, Bethesda, Maryland.

Kirby, J.S., R.J. Evans, and A.D. Fox. 1993. Wintering seaducks in Britain and Ireland: populations, threats, conservation, and research priorities. Aquatic Conservation: Marine and Freshwater Ecosystems 3:105–137.

Laursen, K. 1989. Estimates of sea duck winter populations of the western palaearctic. Danish Review of Game Biology 13(6).

Martin, E. M., and S. M. Carney. 1977. Population ecology of the mallard part IV. A review of duck hunting regulations, activity, and success, with special reference to the mallard. Resource Publication 130, U.S. Fish and Wildlife Service, Washington, D.C.

McKnight, D.E. and I.O. Buss. 1962. Evidence of breeding in yearling female lesser scaup. Journal of Wildlife Management 26:328-329.

Montalbano, F., III, F.A. Johnson, and M.J. Conroy. 1985. Status of wintering ring-necked ducks in the southern Atlantic Flyway. Journal of Wildlife Management 49:543-546.

Nichols, J. D., M. J. Conroy, D. R. Anderson, and K. P. Burnham. 1984. Compensatory mortality in waterfowl populations: a review of the evidence and implications for research and management. Transactions of the North American Wildlife and Natural Resources Conference. 54:535-554.

Office of Migratory Bird Management. 1990. Special scaup seasons and bonus bag limits. Unpublished report. U.S. Fish and Wildlife Service, Laurel, Maryland.

Palmer, R.S. Editor. 1976. Handbook of North American birds, Volume 3: Waterfowl. Yale University Press, New Haven, Connecticut.

Patterson, J. H. 1979. Can ducks be managed by regulation? Transactions of the North American Wildlife and Natural Resources Conference. 44:130-139.

Reynolds, R. E. 1987. Breeding duck population, production and habitat surveys, 1979-85. Transactions of the North American Wildlife and Natural Resources Conference 52:186-205.

Sauer, J. R., S. Schwartz, and B. Hoover. 1996. The Christmas Bird Count Home Page. Version 95.1. U.S. Geological Survey, Laurel, Maryland. http://www.mbr.nbs.gov.

Serie, J. and B. Cruz. 1997. Atlantic Flyway waterfowl harvest and population survey data. Unpublished report, U.S. Fish and Wildlife Service, Laurel, Maryland.

Sharp, D.E. 1997. Central Flyway harvest and population survey data book. Unpublished report, U.S. Fish and Wildlife Service, Denver, Colorado.

Smith, G. 1995. A critical review of the aerial and ground surveys of breeding waterfowl in North America. Biological Science Report Number 5. U.S. Department of the Interior, National Biological Service. Washington, D.C.

Trauger, D.L. 1971. Population ecology of lesser scaup (Aythya affinis) is subarctic taiga. Ph.D. Dissertation. Iowa State University, Ames.

U.S. Fish and Wildlife Service. 1986. North American Waterfowl Management Plan. U.S. Fish and Wildlife Service, Washington, D.C.

U.S. Fish and Wildlife Service. 1994. 1994 Update to the North American Waterfowl Management Plan. U.S. Fish and Wildlife Service, Washington, D.C.

Wilkins, K.A., M.C. Otto, and J.A. Dubovsky. 1998. Trends in duck breeding populations, 1955-1998. Unpublished Administrative Report, U.S. Fish and Wildlife Service. Laurel, Maryland.

www.ingramcontent.com/pod-product-compliance
Lightning Source LLC
Chambersburg PA
CBHW080553290526
45790CB00006B/2640